PROVERBS

by

Ed Brown & Nick Chapman

2019 One Stone Press.
All rights reserved. No part of this book may be reproduced in any form without written permission of the publisher.

Published by:
One Stone Press
979 Lovers Lane
Bowling Green, KY 42103

Printed in the United States of America

ISBN: 978-1-941422-46-5

Supplemental Materials Available:

~ Answer Key

~ Downloadable PDF

www.onestone.com

1.800.428.0121

www.onestone.com

CONTENTS

Lesson 1	Studying Proverbs	5
Lesson 2	Wisdom vs Folly	11
Lesson 3	Parents and Their Children	17
Lesson 4	Building Good Relationships	23
Lesson 5	Money Matters	29
Lesson 6	Spotting a Fool	37
Lesson 7	Poverty and Wealth	45
Lesson 8	Aware vs Impaired	51
Lesson 9	Pride and Humility	59
Lesson 10	A Worthy Woman	65
Lesson 11	Authority	71
Lesson 12	Seeing Jesus in Proverbs	77
Lesson 13	Awe for God	83

Lesson 1

STUDYING PROVERBS

There Is a War out There

There has been a struggle for the heart of man since the Garden of Eden. You are at the age where you have entered into the same war every human must face: the choice between God and Satan, right and wrong, wisdom and foolishness. Solomon recognized that even everyday tasks and problems could affect the path we take in this life. So, in his wisdom (and by the inspiration of God), he penned most of the book of Proverbs.

The Bible identifies Solomon as the author in the first verse, "The proverbs of Solomon, the son of David, king of Israel." This book is Solomon's instruction manual to his sons on how to live life in a way that matches how God wants people to behave daily. Throughout the book, you will see his advice on issues you may not even consider important to your spirituality, like money, authority, relationships, humility, and fools. But you will also see him discuss wisdom, marriage, pride, and arrogance. Soon, you will recognize the choice that has been laid before us all: do I choose wisdom or folly (foolishness)?

Our answer to this question will determine whether we win daily battles and, ultimately, whether we win or lose the war that is waged on our souls. In the short term, our answer will help us live a more problem-free life if we gain the wisdom of God. Proverbs 3:1-2 states, "My son, do not forget my law, but let your heart keep my commands; for length of days and long life and peace

Key Verse

The horse is prepared for the day of battle, but deliverance is of the Lord.

- Proverbs 21:31

they will add to you." In the end, however, our answer will determine our spiritual life or death. Proverbs 8:35-36 warns, "For whoever finds me finds life, and obtains favor from the Lord; but he who sins against me wrongs his own soul; all those who hate me love death."

In the next few lessons, we will look at ways to prepare for this struggle. What if we knew ahead of time what the enemy was going to do? What if we knew beforehand the strategy that would guarantee us victory? Knowing this would give us an advantage! Our lessons will come from the thirty-one chapters of Proverbs. They will tell us all about the characteristics of the enemy: deceit, immorality, laziness, irresponsibility, and more. It will also give us the characteristics of the victor: loving your neighbor, working hard for a living, and keeping yourself morally righteous. Having knowledge of these characteristics will help us choose the kind of person we want to be, and gaining the wisdom to apply them will give us victory in the battle of life.

Look at Proverbs 1:7:

> The fear of the Lord is the
> beginning of knowledge,
> But fools despise wisdom and
> instruction.

Solomon was the wisest man in the Old Testament when he wrote most of the Proverbs. In the first chapter, he tells us where knowledge begins: "the fear of the Lord." To fear the Lord does not mean to be afraid of Him because He can punish us; it also means we respect Him because He is our Father, we love Him because He gives us life, we honor Him because He is powerful, and we glorify Him because He is righteous. The Word of God (our Bible) tells us all about Him, and Solomon said this is where knowledge begins.

Questions

1. Describe in your own words why having knowledge is important. _____

   _____

   _____

   _____

2. Who is the author of Proverbs? _____

   _____

3. Who is the author addressing as the audience of his proverbs (Prov. 1:4)? __

   _____

4. What should the "fear of the Lord" produce? _____

   _____

   _____

What Is a Proverb?

A proverb is a short saying that makes you think about a true principle in life. Proverbs are easy to remember and memorize so you can tell others, and the word "proverb" is derived from the Hebrew word *mashal*, literally referring to a brief sentence of wisdom. Sometimes, they are humorous, but proverbs are not intended to be just for entertainment. Their purpose is to offer useful advice on how to live righteously in this world and how to build character that is becoming of a godly person.

The Proverbs are also written in a poetic format. God uses different ways to teach us His word in the Bible. At times, it is in a story format, like Moses and the burning bush. Sometimes, we read about God giving His instructions through a direct command, like when He gave the children of Israel the Ten Commandments. God also uses poetry. The Book of Proverbs is a special kind of poetry that was popular in the ancient Near Eastern culture of that period in history. It is not like most of our modern poems because it does not rhyme or use the structure we are familiar with today.

Proverbs is not the only book that contains poetry. Ecclesiastes, Song of Solomon, Job, and Psalms are all written in poetic form. Also, the prophets wrote much of their prophecies in poems. In fact, about one-third of the Old Testament is written in a poetic format. Therefore, it is important for us to recognize poetry when we are reading scripture, so we get the clear meaning of what God is teaching us. Poems use imagery to make a point. What is the image you think of when you read, "Roses are red, violets are blue..."? You think of pretty flowers, right? And that makes you think of pleasant things. The poetry in Proverbs works the same way.

Look at Proverbs 25:28:

> Whoever has no rule over
> His own spirit
> Is like a city broken down,
> Without walls.

What image comes to your mind when you read "a city broken down, without walls"? Do you think of a city that is in trouble? God wants us to think of our spirit as being in trouble if we do not have rule over it. Recognizing poetry and the images in it are important in helping us understand the message God has for us.

Questions

5. Using Proverbs 10:26, what are the images and the lesson? _____
   _____
   _____
   _____

6. How much of the Old Testament is written in poetic form? _____
   _____

How Do We Read Proverbs?

The Book of Proverbs is full of everyday instructions. These instructions contain the knowledge God wants us to have so we can live every day pleasing Him. Each morning brings a new battle, and we need God's instruction on how to conquer the challenges we face. Most of the proverbs are very short—only one verse with a couple of lines. Many times, two lines will form a couplet. The lines will be related to each other, but the second line will usually add words that make the meaning richer and more valuable.

Look at Proverbs 1:5:

> A wise man will hear and
> increase learning,
> And a man of understanding
> will attain wise counsel.

This proverb is one verse long and made up of a couplet. It is telling us how a wise man will act; he will "hear and increase learning." But the second part of the verse adds to these instructions by telling us he "will attain wise counsel." The second part gives us more information about how to "increase learning." Both lines are talking about the wise man, and it is important to read them together.

Consider Proverbs 12:2:

> A good man obtains favor
> from the Lord.
> But a man of wicked intentions
> He will condemn.

The second part of this couplet is opposite from the first. It talks about how God will treat the "good man" versus the "man of wicked intentions." But it is still important to read them together to get the full impact of God's authority.

Questions

7. Using Proverbs 17:20-28, give an example of a couplet that talks about the same thing in both lines and an example of a couplet that contains opposite thoughts. _____
_____
_____

8. How many lines does a couplet contain? _____
_____

9. Do couplets always contain opposite thoughts? _____
_____

If you have not noticed yet, life can be hard. Being a follower of God certainly helps give us focus, but we are not promised a problem-free life on this earth. We all have to deal with people we do not like. We all face embarrassing moments and painful memories from poor choices.

We all face trials. James 1:2-3 states, "My brethren, count it all joy when you fall into various trials, knowing that the testing of your faith produces patience." How does God expect us to get through it all? By seeking and obtaining His wisdom. The study of Proverbs is a good first step in becoming a wise follower of God.

"Life isn't easy...Sometimes, we wake up in the morning and see the day as a series of obstacles to be avoided...The Bible has a word to describe the person who navigates life well; that word is 'wise.'"

– Tremper Longman III

Lesson 2

WISDOM vs. FOLLY
The Battle for Our Soul

Let the Battle Begin

Sound dramatic? Because it is! The choice between wisdom and folly is the main theme that binds all the proverbs in this book. Another way to think of this is purity versus immorality. Remember the warning at the beginning of the book: "The fear of the Lord is the beginning of knowledge, but fools despise wisdom and instruction," (Proverbs 1:7). No one wants to be a fool, but if we lack wisdom and knowledge, we may not realize that a fool is what we are.

In order to help us understand this struggle, the writer gives us two characters that personify wisdom and folly. "Personification" is giving human characteristics to something that is not human. "Wisdom" and "Folly" are portrayed as two women. Since the book of Proverbs is addressed to young men, this would have a natural appeal, especially since these women are trying to get a young man's attention. They are both trying to get him to establish a close relationship with them.

Just as a close relationship with a good friend has an influence on your behavior and character, so too will an association with either Wisdom or Folly. But the choice between these two will impact the rest of your life. That is why there is a struggle between the two; they are fighting over your eternal soul. Listen carefully to the words of Solomon to see which of these two offer you the best option for your future.

Key Verse

The fear of the Lord is the beginning of knowledge, but fools despise wisdom and instruction.

- Proverbs 1:7

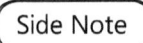

Just because Proverbs is addressed to young men in no way means that it does not apply to women or older men. All books in the Bible had an original audience that was not us, but God intended all scripture to guide His children. There will be more on this later.

Questions

1. What is wisdom to you? _____
   _____
   _____

2. Think of someone who shows wisdom and write down what you think makes them wise. _____
   _____
   _____

3. Write down something foolish you have done in the past and state why it was foolish. _____
   _____
   _____

4. Why do you think Solomon portrayed Wisdom and Folly as women? _____
   _____
   _____

Who Are These Women?

We are first introduced to the woman Wisdom in Proverbs 1:20-33. What does she have to offer that would make someone want to establish a long-time relationship with her? The best way to get to know someone is to observe their character and companions. Proverbs 8:12 tells us, "I, wisdom, dwell with prudence, and find out knowledge and discretion." Verse 14 states, "Counsel is mine, and sound wisdom; I am understanding, I have strength."

First, Wisdom's seeking out knowledge and discretion. You know what knowledge is, but what about discretion? Discretion is the "quality of behaving or speaking in such a way as to avoid causing offense or revealing private information." In other words, Wisdom is someone who's striving to know a lot and is someone you can completely trust with your heart. Prudence is her companion. Prudence is "having the quality to act with or show care and thought for the future." Wisdom is not just concerned about today; she is looking ahead and carefully planning her future.

Wisdom goes on to describe herself as having counsel. Counsel is "guidance or recommendations concerning prudent future action, usually given by someone who is knowledgeable" (like a guidance counselor at school). Wisdom stresses that she is understanding. Not only does she have the knowledge, but she knows how best to use it. To top it off, she proclaims she has strength. This is not physical strength; it is strength of character and integrity.

These traits may not be in the top-ten list of characteristics a young man looks for in a woman. But to those that yield to her teaching and stay with her, what will they gain? We are told they will gain riches, honor, and righteousness (Proverbs 8:18). We also see the type of people that associate with her because of what she has to offer (Proverbs 8:15-16):

> [15] By me kings reign,
> And rulers decree justice.
> [16] By me princes rule, and nobles,
> All the judges of the earth.

Kings, rulers, princes, nobles, and judges are very distinguished and honored company, and they all use wisdom to help them succeed in their roles. Also important is that Wisdom will lead her followers to a life with fewer problems and greater godly potential. "But whoever listens to me will dwell safely, and will be secure, without fear of evil," (Proverbs 1:33). Solomon showed he already had a wise heart because he chose for God to grant him knowledge and understanding, and God was pleased with his choice. "Behold, I have done according to your words; see, I have given you a wise and understanding heart, so that there has not been anyone like you before you, nor shall any like you arise after you. And I have also given you what you have not asked: both riches and honor, so that there shall not be anyone like you among the kings all your days," (1 Kings 3:12-13).

The woman "Folly" is described in Proverbs 9:13-18. She, too, calls out to young men who are starting on the path of life. She is described as "clamorous" (9:13), which means "loud while being rowdy or very insistent." Notice the only other characteristic used to describe her: "She is simple, and knows nothing" (9:13). What is her message to those listening? Folly urges, "Whoever is simple, let him turn in here," (9:16).

See what she offers to those who heed her call: "Stolen water is sweet, and bread eaten in secret is pleasant." This is not a call to improve one's character but a simple call to live for the moment. The lure of doing something wrong can be appealing to all but especially to young people. Unfortunately, this is the type of woman that often catches men's eyes. These are the types of temptations that capture the hearts of young people even today. Folly is especially calling to young people. She wants to trap you before you know better. Learning about her and the dangers she poses to your life is the first step toward wisdom.

Questions

5. Do your friends influence how you act? In what ways? _____
_____
_____

6. Friends influence how one acts. List ways your friends have influenced your actions for good or bad. _____
_____
_____

7. How has a "wise" friend or adult made a good change in your life? _____
_____
_____

The True Meaning

It should not take long to figure out there's a deeper meaning to the struggle between the wise and the foolish, between the pure and the immoral. The woman Wisdom is representative of God's wisdom. Note how Wisdom calls from the heights of the city, where her home is located (9:1-3). At the time this was written, the people would place their temples and altars upon the high places. The LORD God has called His people to hear His words of wisdom and obey them.

The phrase "The fear of the Lord is the beginning of wisdom" from our key verse in Proverbs 1:7 is repeated here in Proverbs 9:10. When a Bible student finds a repeated phrase or idea while reading the Bible, it is called an "inclusio." Think of an inclusio as a pair of bookends; the material between them is related to this repeated theme. God is telling not only young men but everyone, that fearing Him is of the utmost importance. It is easy to understand the attraction young men have for women. So, God used this idea to emphasize how important it is for His people to seek Him and the wisdom He provides for a life with fewer problems.

But what distracts us from hearing God's call? The woman Folly distracts us. She calls with the allurements this world provides. Notice that her home is also in the high places, "on a seat by the highest places of the city, to call to those who pass by" (9:14, 15). The children of Israel were plagued with false idols on the high places as well, and these idols caused the destruction of many. But there is only one reward for the fool that follows her. "But he does not know that the dead are there, that her guests are in the depths of hell," (9:18). References to a harlot and adulterous woman are sprinkled throughout the book as well, and all point to God's children being unfaithful to Him because they have acted like fools and have denied Him.

Questions

8. As a young person, what major decisions will you make in the next few years?

_____

_____

_____

9. How could following Folly make the decisions in your life harder? _____

_____

_____

10. How could heeding Wisdom make the decisions in your life easier? _____

_____

_____

"It is no accident that Proverbs routinely uses the image of a seductive, adulterous woman as the figurative personification of the concept of folly (9:13-18). 'Lady Folly' appears attractive and high class, but in reality, she is only sin and destruction attired in fine clothing.

"Just as Proverbs personifies the concept of foolishness as an adulteress, it personifies wisdom as a virtuous woman (1:20-33; 8:1-9:6). By allowing oneself to be attracted to 'Lady Wisdom,' and by joining oneself to her—that is, by allowing discretion to be one's constant companion—a man can more easily resist the temptations of adultery and every other kind of folly (7:4-5)."

– Marty Pickup

Lesson 3

PARENTS AND THEIR CHILDREN

How God Intended It to Be

When you watch television or movies, how often do you see the parents portrayed as "not too bright" and the kids as having everything figured out? It is an unfortunate trend in today's culture, and it usually beats up on fathers the most. I have to admit, fathers do make big mistakes at times, but we can never forget that they have more experience and wisdom than children.

Remember, the book of Proverbs was written by a father to his son. "My son, hear the instruction of your father, and do not forsake the law of your mother" (Proverbs 1:8). Solomon wanted to pass on some of life's lessons to his child. Note the second part of this verse emphasizes the importance of a mother's instruction as well. Most parents want to teach their children as much as possible to help them avoid the mistakes they might have made. One of the parents' main jobs is to prepare their children to become adults and function well in society.

Think about God and how He talks about His relationship with mankind. He calls us His children, and He's our Heavenly Father. In the Old Testament, the children of Israel had that special relationship with Him. "Yet the number of the children of Israel shall be as the sand of the sea, which cannot be measured or numbered... There it shall be said to them, 'You are sons of the living God,'" (Hosea 10:1). In the New Testament, we see that all believers

Key Verse

Train up a child in the way he should go, and when he is old he will not depart from it.

- Proverbs 22:6

can now have that special title. Galatians 3:26 states, "For you are all sons of God through faith in Christ Jesus."

The greatest responsibility parents have is to raise their children as God intended. Our key verse Proverbs 22:6 states, "Train up a child in the way he should go, and when he is old he will not depart from it." God wants parents to teach their children to love, respect, and honor Him above all others. There are horrible consequences when parents do not train their children to fear and love God. Hosea 4:1 reads:

> Hear the word of the Lord, You children of Israel,
> For the Lord brings a charge against the inhabitants of the land:
> "There is no truth or mercy or knowledge of God in the land."

Later, Hosea proclaims, "My people are destroyed for lack of knowledge," (Hosea 4:6).

Questions

1. How do your parents help teach you about God? _____
   _____
   _____

2. What did God promise would happen if His people did not obey Him? List at least three terrible things God would do. (See Deuteronomy 28:15-68) ____
   _____
   _____
   _____
   _____

3. What is a parent's greatest responsibility? _____
   _____
   _____

The Role of the Parent

What does it mean to "train up a child in the way he should go?" Solomon partially answers that question in the verse we quoted earlier: "My son, hear the instruction of your father, and do not forsake the law of your mother," (Proverbs 1:8). Let us start with instruction and see how Proverbs helps parents raise their children.

Instruction

Parents are to instruct their children. They are to instill godly values, set boundaries, teach manners, demand respect, and see to their children's spiritual and secular education. If you view Proverbs as a "how-to" book on living in this world, you will see the advice by Solomon for all these areas, but the fear and knowledge of God are the key elements. Proverbs 2: 1, 5 state: "My son, if you receive my words, and treasure my commands within you…Then you will understand the fear of the Lord, and find the knowledge of God."

Parents instruct their children by:

- Speaking and Teaching: "Hear, my children, the instruction of a father, and give attention to know understanding," (Proverbs 4:1). Parents give verbal instruction and teaching. Although it may not be what we want to hear, it is often what we need to hear.

- Repetition (Reminding Them): "My son, do not forget my law, but let your heart keep my commands," (Proverbs 3:1). This is why your parents tend to say the same thing over and over. They want to make sure you take their instruction to heart until it becomes second nature to you.

- Setting an Example: "But as for you, speak the things which are proper for sound doctrine: that the older men be sober, reverent, temperate, sound in faith, in love, in patience; the older women likewise, that they be reverent in behavior, not slanderers, not given to much wine, teachers of good things," (Titus 2:1-2). We borrowed this verse from the New Testament because it emphasizes the importance of real, life examples and the impact they can have on the younger generation.

Discipline: Instruction with a Sting

Parents are to discipline their children. Yep, you knew this one was coming. There are several verses related to discipline that seem abusive in the light of modern thinking. But a parent using corporal punishment (spanking) is not wrong in itself. When a child outgrows that stage, parents need to discipline (i.e., remove privileges) in a way that makes their point.

Proverbs 23:13 says, "Do not withhold correction from a child, for if you beat him with a rod, he will not die."

You may be wondering, "Why should parents use discipline at all?" Because, in our hearts, we all know we need boundaries to keep us from misbehaving. And your parents have more wisdom than you do because they have lived through being whatever age you are. They have been there and done that.

The motivation for discipline is love, although it may be hard for you to believe. Solomon said, "He who spares his rod hates his son, but he who loves him disciplines him promptly," (Proverbs 13:24). This love is one that wants to keep you from following the wrongful desire of your own heart. Discipline should be used to mold you into an adult that fears God and respects others. We have all seen examples of children who receive no real discipline. We call them brats.

There are tragic examples of fathers who would not discipline their sons. Let us look at the case of Eli, who was a high priest of God. Although Eli did an excellent job helping raise Samuel, he failed miserably with his sons, who were horrible, ungodly men. For the full account, 1 Samuel 2 contains the story, but the main problem was obvious: Now the sons of Eli were corrupt; they did not know the Lord, (1 Samuel 2: 12). Eli failed to "train up a child in the way he should go."

Parents do need to use positive reinforcement (praise and encouragement) as tools too. But their discipline teaches you that there are consequences to wrong behavior—if not in this life, then in the afterlife.

Now, it is your turn. List the benefits of discipline found in the following verses:
- Proverbs 29:15 _____
- Proverbs 22:15 _____
- Proverbs 23:14 _____

The Role of the Child

Children have just as important a role to play in the family. First, know that almost all parents love their children and take pride in having them. To borrow a verse from Psalm 127:3, "Behold, children are a heritage from the Lord, the fruit of the womb is a reward."

But you, as a child, can either bring joy or shame to your house. Proverbs 29:15 says, "The rod and rebuke give wisdom, but a child left to himself brings shame to his mother." Proverbs 15:20 also says, "A wise son makes a father glad, but a foolish man despises his mother."

What a difference gaining wisdom makes in people's lives. How can you as a child help yourself be acceptable in God's eyes? Let us explore.

Listen and Learn

Since your parents are to teach you, the best thing you can do is learn. Again, we can go back to Proverbs 1:8: "My son, hear the instruction of your father, and do not forsake the law of your mother." The teenage years can be the "Age of Eye-Rolling." As teens, we try to spread our wings a bit and rebel some against mom and dad. Their advice may seem a bit old-fashioned and way too restrictive. You may not understand why they prohibit you from doing certain things, thinking they do not understand you. The truth is, they have been teenagers before and know the emotions and difficulties you are going through better than you think. Trust their judgment.

You will rarely hear a grown up mutter, "I wish I'd listened to my parents less." The opposite is true. The older one gets, the more one realizes parents have wisdom and experience and that their teaching can help guide a person through the tough times in life. Learn their wisdom, especially when they are training you in the law of God.

Learn from Discipline

Nobody likes to be disciplined, but it is a part of life. A person can either learn from their mistakes or continue in them. Learning from your errors is a huge step toward gaining wisdom. Your parents' discipline is their attempt at molding you into a better person, just as God's discipline is for guiding His children to repentance and godly behavior.

Accept the punishments you receive, and take them to heart. Do not be like the fool and go right back to doing the wrong thing over and over. "As a dog returns to his own vomit, so a fool repeats his folly," (Proverbs 26:11). Learning not to err is a sign of growing in wisdom and maturity. It is how you develop your own sense of good judgment to guide you through future decisions.

Questions

4. When you have children, will you want them to listen to you? Why? _____
   _____
   _____

5. Why should people obey God? Who is He? _____
   _____
   _____

6. Does God's authority over us have any connection with the parent-child relationship? How? _____
   _____
   _____
   _____

Paul states God's desire for all children best in Ephesians 6:1-3: "Children, obey your parents in the Lord, for this is right. 'Honor your father and mother,' which is the first commandment with promise: 'that it may be well with you and you may live long on the earth.'"

FRIENDS AND NEIGHBORS
Building Good Relationships

Other than your family, with whom do you spend most of your time? Friends. There are also people who live close to you and you see often: neighbors. These two sets of people can have a huge impact on my happiness. God recognizes this and, through Solomon's wisdom, addresses the need to build good relationships with them both.

Friends

Think of some of your favorite friends. What images flash through your head? Usually, we remember good times and laughter. We might also think about our close friends helping us through difficult times and problems in our lives. Proverbs offers valuable advice on friendship because God's aware that humans need and rely on their close friends.

Proverbs 18:24 says, "A man who has friends must himself be friendly, but there is a friend who sticks closer than a brother." Our good friends can often be closer to us than real family members. Being a friend is not a one-way relationship. We must be friendly ourselves to have and keep friends. Let us see what other nuggets of wisdom we can uncover.

Reliable & Honest

All relationships are built on trust. If we discover someone is a habitual liar, we tend to stay away from them

Key Verse

Do not forsake your own friend or your father's friend, nor go to your brother's house in the day of your calamity; better is a neighbor nearby than brother far away.
- Proverbs 27:10

because we can not depend on what they say or do. Trust is even more important in a friendship since we tend to speak openly and more often with a friend. It is valuable to have a friend who knows your secrets and faults but will not gossip about you to others.

Friends must be reliable. Being able to depend on a friend to keep their word is of importance. Nothing can be more frustrating than relying on a friend to show up, and they just do not come or forget. Has this happened to you? Aggravating, isn't it? On the other side, you cannot be one of those friends either. Have you forgotten to show up when needed? Be a reliable friend to keep your loyal friends because you want to be a friend who "sticks closer than a brother."

Friends also need to be honest. Of course, this means not telling each other lies, but it involves more than this. Honesty is an aspect of friendship that can be difficult when it comes to recognizing serious faults in one another and then lovingly trying to correct them. We often overlook the smaller faults of our friends, because that is what friends do. But what if your friend is about to do something you think they should not? Do you stand up to them?

In Proverbs 27:5-6, Solomon says, "Open rebuke is better than love carefully concealed. Faithful are the wounds of a friend, but the kisses of an enemy are deceitful." A rebuke is a sharp disapproval of an action. It is not easy to tell a friend when they are wrong, but sometimes, it is for their good. This "sting" may result in the loss of the friendship, for awhile. You may not have the courage to stop your friend because you are afraid you will lose their friendship. But in time, your friend will hopefully see you had their best interests at heart. "Faithful are the wounds of a friend" who rebukes you. The wounds are the temporary pain you feel when corrected. No one likes being corrected, but we all need to be on occasion. Keep that in mind when a friend corrects you.

Questions

1. Read 1 Kings 12:6-8. Who were good friends to King Rehoboam and who were bad friends? _____
_____
_____

2. What motivation do you think the bad friends had for their advice? _____
   _____
   _____

3. Find a proverb for your answer to question two. _____
   _____

4. List an example of a time you rebuked a friend or when you were rebuked. (Be prepared to share with the class.) _____
   _____
   _____
   _____

Mutual Growth

The right kind of friend will help you grow stronger. When a friend rebukes or corrects a behavior of yours, it can shape you into a better person. Growth can also occur through mutual experiences, which allow you to share time, thoughts, and opinions. You know how a friendly debate with a friend can sway each of you to the other's point of view. The trick is being with the right kind of friend that helps guide you toward God and not this earth.

Proverbs 13:20 says, "He who walks with wise men will be wise, but the companion of fools will be destroyed." If you want to follow the path of wisdom God calls us to find, make friends with those who seek the same thing. Once again, we see that hanging around with fools just does not pay off.

But there is an even deeper opportunity for personal growth with a close friend. Consider the unlikely friendship between David and Jonathan. David braved King Saul's hatred for him, and Jonathan was willing to bear the displeasure of his father. The two of them grew so close that they were ready to face death for one another. Think of the impact Jonathan had on the eventual king of Israel, for David will always be remembered as "a man after God's own heart."

This strengthening of character during tough times is summed up best by Solomon in Proverbs 27:17: "As iron sharpens iron, so a man sharpens the countenance of his friend." It takes a stone as hard as iron to sharpen an iron blade. In the same way, it takes a friend of equal or greater character to help shape you into a better person. Can your friends depend on your character to help them grow too?

Friends to Avoid

We have already seen that fools are always to be avoided. Proverbs also warns of people with quick tempers. Association with these friends might get you into bad situations because of their anger, and it might just rub off on you.

Proverbs 22:24-25 says, "Make no friendship with an angry man, and with a furious man do not go, lest you learn his ways and set a snare for your soul."

Questions

5. Read 1 Samuel 20.

6. What was Jonathan willing to do for David? _____

_____

_____

7. What was David willing to let Jonathan do to him for their friendship? _____

_____

_____

8. How deep was the love between these two friends? _____

_____

9. Based on what we have studied, would King Saul have made a good friend? Why or why not? _____

_____

_____

_____

(Side Note)

Many homosexual activists today try to make the friendship between David and Jonathan into something that was not pure. Men of our culture show friendship in different ways. To this day, you will still find men in Europe and the Middle East who embrace and kiss and are nothing more than friends. But in any culture, you will find close friends who are willing to die for each other.

Neighbors

The average American moves eleven or more times during his life. Our neighbors are constantly changing. But being a good neighbor is a virtue, wherever you are—especially as teenagers. If you show wisdom and godly virtue, you might be just the right influence to draw others to God.

The best definition of "neighbor" comes from Jesus himself in the parable of the Good Samaritan in Luke 10:29-37. In the end, the Samaritan proved to be a good neighbor who showed mercy on the beaten traveler. In other words, we are to do good deeds and watch daily for those whom we come into contact. This would be especially true of our neighbors who are close to our home.

Solomon tells us "how" to be a good neighbor by telling us "what not to do." He gives a list of things not to do to our neighbors to remain at peace with them.

- Do not refuse to loan something to your neighbor if you can help (3:28).
- Do not be a false witness against your neighbor (24:28).
- Work out your differences without going to court (25:8-10).
- Do not overstay your welcome or linger too long at your neighbor's house (25:17).
- Do not play rotten pranks on your neighbor and then claim you were only joking (26:18-19).

In everyday language, this translates to: do not be selfish, do not lie, do not pick fights, and do not be a pest—all sound advice from a very wise man. Why should we want to be friends with our neighbors? We have already mentioned you could be a good influence and lead them to God. Another reason is that God wants us to be a good neighbor; that is why Solomon gave us these warnings.

There are other valuable benefits to having a good relationship with your neighbors. Solomon said in Proverbs 3:29, "Do not devise evil against your neighbor, for he dwells by you for safety's sake."

People live close to each other because there is safety in numbers. Good neighbors look after each other's homes, belongings, pets, and children. It is comforting for your parents to know someone is watching.

Neighbors can also offer you support, just as a friend would. Note the last phrase in our key verse (Proverbs 27:10): "Better is a neighbor nearby than a brother far away." When tragedy strikes, neighbors are there to help and comfort you. Yes, your church family is also there, as they should be, but a good neighbor supports you just like family. Are you the type of neighbor that will help those in need?

Questions

10. In the parable of the Good Samaritan, what was surprising about the men who did not help? _____

_____

11. List some ways you could be a good neighbor in your neighborhood. _____

_____

_____

_____

12. Read Proverbs 14:21. How important is it to God that we're good neighbors?

_____

_____

You are never too young to start being a good neighbor. Sometimes, young people are fooled into thinking, "I'll be different when I grow up." But whatever we do to train our hearts when we are young shapes what we are when we are older.

Solomon knew this and said in Proverbs 20:11, "Even a child is known by his deeds, whether what he does is pure and right." In Ecclesiastes 12:1, Solomon also said, "Remember now your Creator in the days of your youth..."

Lesson 5

MONEY MATTERS
Our Material Blessings

Does Money Matter?

Money is a part of life. There is no escaping this fundamental law of human existence. So, do you think God is concerned with how His children view money matters? You bet He is. There is no richer place to find advice and direction about the practicalities of dealing with wealth than right here in Proverbs.

Proverbs 10:22 states, "The blessing of the Lord makes one rich, and He adds no sorrow with it." The Bible is full of examples of God blessing His children with material goods. In Genesis 12:2, God promised Abraham, "I will bless you and make your name great." In Deuteronomy 28:2, the Lord also assures the children of Israel that they will be blessed in the Promised Land if they continued to obey: "And all these blessings shall come upon you and overtake you, because you obey the voice of the Lord your God." But as we go through this lesson, you will find that an abundance of material blessings are not always guaranteed in this life. What is true though is that God will provide for His children.

Of course, money, as we think of it today, was not exactly the only thing used in Old Testament times, but people have always exchanged their goods and services to get others' goods and services. The accumulation of "earthly things" is what we call wealth. The lack of those same items is what we call poverty. On which side of that line do

Key Verse

The blessing of the Lord makes one rich, and He adds no sorrow with it.

- Proverbs 10:22

you want to be? Easy—no one wants to be poor. But as we will see in this lesson, there are worse things than being poor.

Questions

1. Do you think life is easier or harder when you are wealthy? Why? _____
   _____
   _____

2. How can wealth be used for good? How can it be used for evil? _____
   _____
   _____
   _____

3. Give your opinion on what Jesus meant when He said, "It is easier for a camel to go through the eye of a needle than for a rich man to enter the kingdom of God." (Mark 10:25) _____
   _____
   _____
   _____

What Is Going on Here?

As we study some of the principles of wealth and poverty, we are going to run across verses that seem to contradict one another. For instance, compare these two verses:

- "The blessing of the Lord makes one rich, and He adds no sorrow with it," (Proverbs 10:22).
- "Better is the poor who walks in his integrity than one perverse in his ways, though he be rich," (Proverbs 22:6).

The first verse seems to say God will bless the righteous with wealth, and then it turns around in the second verse and says an honest, poor man is better off than a wicked, rich man. Why didn't God make the poor honest, man rich? Why was the evil man rich at all? The answer is because the proverbs are principles and not absolute truths.

If you follow the advice God lays out in Proverbs, you will live a life that is more problem-free than a life of one who is wicked. The godly person is always rich because he belongs to God, being His child. The godly are also blessed with a heavenly home when this life is over.

A great example of this is Jesus's parable of the Rich Man and Lazarus in Luke 16:19-31. Here, Jesus presents an example of a rich man who prospered while on Earth but did not use his money in a godly way or live according to God's word. At his gate was a poor beggar, who must have remained a faithful child of God, even in his horrible condition. At death, we see the poor man received his eternal blessing with Abraham, yet the rich man was in torment.

Questions

4. How do you feel when evil people seem to be blessed? After you write your response, read Psalm 73:1-3. _____

_____

_____

5. Why would God allow a faithful servant to suffer poverty (Eph. 2:8-9)? _____

_____

_____

6. How well did the Rich Man's wealth serve him after he died in Luke 16? ___

_____

_____

The Benefits of Godly Living

Even though there are no guarantees, living by the godly principles within God's word can help make you successful in this life. Just being honest, polite, and punctual will help you succeed in the workplace. So often, you will see fellow workers who are disrespectful, lazy, and dishonest. In your lifetime, you will see many of these people fired because employers want workers they can trust to do a good job. In Proverbs, we see a connection with proper behavior toward God and the blessings He gives His children.

Note Proverbs 3:9-10: "Honor the Lord with your possessions, and with the firstfruits of all your increase; so your barns will be filled with plenty, and your vats will overflow with new wine." Even though this references an agricultural setting, the connection is made that God blesses those who honor Him.

Also, note Proverbs 13:11: "Wealth gained by dishonesty will be diminished, but he who gathers by labor will increase." Here is one of those apparent contradictions. The first part of the verse shows that dishonest people can obtain wealth, but in the end, it will not last. But focus on the principle in the second part, where the person who honestly labors (just plain hard work) will have an increase in his wealth.

Imagine, hard work equals financial gain. Do not be tempted later in life by schemes and tricks that say you can get rich quickly with little or no work or sacrifice. That type of effort usually falls into the category of "wealth gained by dishonesty," and people who fall for these traps usually end up losing a lot of their money because of an unwise decision. God wants His people to be productive with their time. They need to provide for their own needs, and if God blesses some with abundance, He expects them to use it wisely.

Questions

7. Does God guarantee that His children will be rich in this life? Why or why not?

   _____
   _____

8. Will God always provide for His children (See Matthew 6:25-34)? How? _____

   _____
   _____

9. If God provides, does that mean I never have to work (See 1 Tim. 5:8)? Why? __

   _____
   _____

10. Ask your parents to tell you about a "get rich quick" scheme they have heard.

    _____
    _____
    _____

A Fool & His Money Are Soon Parted

Proverbs 21:17 states, "He who loves pleasure will be a poor man; He who loves wine and oil will not be rich."

A foolish man who comes into wealth will usually not be able to hang onto it because he lacks good judgment. This example in Proverbs shows a person who foolishly spends all his money on pleasing his desires. He does not invest, he does not save, and he does not give back to God or share it with others. This fool's money will vanish as quickly as he can make it. This shows another advantage to gaining godly wisdom: it helps prevent you from making poor decisions.

There is another quality a fool possesses that usually leads him down the path of poverty. In Proverbs, foolishness is often tied to being lazy. Let us look at an example in Proverbs 10:4-5:

> [4] He who has a slack hand becomes poor,
> But the hand of the diligent makes rich.
> [5] He who gathers in summer is a wise son;
> He who sleeps in harvest is a son who causes shame.

A slack hand is one that is not working. The wise young man is busy doing good labor and gaining wisdom by his actions. A lazy son is foolish, preferring sleep to work; he will cause shame and poverty. Take these verses to heart at your age. Everyone admires a hard worker (except maybe a lazy fool). If you can train yourself to be a good worker while you are young, it will serve you well in God's kingdom and the workplace—not to mention school.

Borrowing Money

It is clear that Proverbs strongly advises against borrowing more money than a person can pay back. Proverbs 22:26-27 says, "Do not be one of those who shakes hands in a pledge, one of those who is surety for debts; if you have nothing with which to pay, why should he take away your bed from under you?"

Our culture and economy are built on credit. You will probably receive your first credit card application before you finish high school and the thought of spending a large amount of money to buy things you want can be appealing. Plus, you only have to pay it back in small amounts. This thought process has driven many young people (and young married couples) right into bankruptcy. Credit card companies charge outrageous interest rates and in the end, you lose some of your wealth just to the bank for the privilege of using their card. Learn this lesson early, and you will be more secure concerning money matters later in life.

Questions

11. Read Proverbs 6:6-11. What lesson should we learn from the ant? _____
   _____
   _____

12. Do you try to "get out of work" when you're home? Do you think your parents notice? Do you think God notices? Are you being wise? _____
   _____
   _____

13. Read Proverbs 22:7. What's the danger of borrowing money? _____
   _____
   _____

What Is the Bottom Line?

The bottom line in business is the outcome of all your hard work. So, what is the bottom line of living a godly life? It is not necessarily earthly wealth, as we have seen; it is something of much more value.

Proverbs 13:7 states, "There is one who makes himself rich, yet has nothing; and one who makes himself poor, yet has great riches." How could a rich man have nothing? And how could a poor man have great riches? Let's see.

Proverbs 15:16 says, "Better is a little with the fear of the Lord, than great treasure with trouble." Obtaining godly wisdom provides a reward of peace in this life. The apostle Paul tells the Philippian brethren that "the peace of God, which surpasses all understanding, will guard your hearts and minds through Christ Jesus" (Phil. 4:7).

Finally, Proverbs 11:4 proclaims, "Riches do not profit in the day of wrath, but righteousness delivers from death." When the last day comes, a rich man's wealth won't buy him any favors with the Lord, but the wise and righteous person will find favor in God's eyes. There's no shame in not being wealthy in this life. God doesn't measure the quality of a person by the accumulation of material wealth; God judges the heart.

Remember Proverbs 10:22: "The blessing of the Lord makes one rich, and He adds no sorrow with it."

Lesson 6

SPOTTING A FOOL
A Wise Approach to Dealing with Fools

Out of the blue, someone around you says or does something incredibly foolish. What do you do? Do you try to correct them? Do you strongly disagree with them? Or do you just ignore them? Does Proverbs even address an everyday occurrence like this? Of course it does as our key verse demonstrates.

Several verses throughout Proverbs help us identify fools by telling what they do, warning of the consequences of their actions, and showing how you can deal with them. Let's begin with what makes a fool a *fool*.

Characteristics of a Fool

Why is a fool a *fool*? Is it lack of mental ability that forces someone to be a fool? No. Proverbs 1:7 is a verse we should all be familiar with during this study, and it tells us there is only one reason a person is a fool: they choose to be. This verse states, "The fear of the Lord is the beginning of knowledge, but fools despise wisdom and instruction."

It is this refusal to seek wisdom or be taught that sets fools apart from someone who honestly desires to become wise in this life. Fools refuse to believe wisdom offers them anything they need. On top of this, Proverbs 18:2 says, "A fool has no delight in understanding, but in expressing his own heart."

The fool just does not take any pleasure in gaining understanding. He is more interested in self and not others.

Key Verse

"Do not answer a fool according to his folly, lest you also be like him."

- Proverbs 26:4

Now, we can take a look at some more characteristics that will help you identify a fool.

A Fool is Angry

Anger is defined as a strong feeling of annoyance, displeasure, or hostility. It is an emotion we all experience often and is not necessarily a problem by itself. Even Jesus showed anger during his time here on earth (Mark 3:5; Matthew 21:12-13). So, what sets a fool's anger apart from ours? It is his inability to control that emotion.

Look at these examples:

- "A fool's wrath is known at once, but a prudent man covers shame," (Proverbs 12:16).
- "A fool's lips enter into contention, and his mouth calls for blows," (Proverbs 14:6-7).
- "A fool vents all his feelings, but a wise man holds them back," (Proverbs 20:3).

A fool not only vents his anger, but he also looks for a fight. His anger is quick to surface, and instead of trying to suppress it, he fans the flames of fury. Anger quickly leads to sin if left unchecked. Paul told the Ephesians, "'Be angry, and do not sin': do not let the sun go down on your wrath, nor give place to the devil" (Ephesians 4:26-27). It is easy for Satan to tempt an angry heart, so fools set themselves up for disaster.

A Fool Hates Authority

What happens when people ignore the law and do their own thing? Chaos. You can see examples of this even today during natural disasters when people loot and steal because there is no one to stop them. Society is built on laws and moral codes so that we will respect others and their belongings. Police officers and the legal system enforce laws for everyone's protection and security.

God is the ultimate authority. He still allows governments and powers to come into power today to serve His purpose (Romans 13:1). He set men as the head of the household and parents as the natural leaders and trainers of their children (Ephesians 5:23, 6:1). God desires obedient hearts. After Saul had disobeyed God, Samuel told him, "Behold, to obey is better than sacrifice" (1 Samuel 15:22). Jesus said, "If you love Me, keep My commandments" (John 14:23). So, would it be wise or foolish to submit to authority?

Proverbs tells us:

- "A fool despises his father's instruction, but he who receives correction is prudent," (Proverbs 15:5).
- "A wise son makes a father glad, but a foolish man despises his mother," (Proverbs 15:20).

And David said, "The fool has said in his heart, 'There is no God,'" (Psalm 14:1).

A Fool Thinks He Is Always Right

A fool has built up himself as the authority on all matters. Since he hates authority, he must place himself as the peak of perfection. This would be another reason why he hates instruction because who can teach someone who knows it all?

Proverbs teaches:

- "The way of a fool is right in his own eyes, but he who heeds counsel is wise," (Proverbs 12:15).
- "He who trusts in his own heart is a fool, but whoever walks wisely will be delivered," (Proverbs 28:26).

On top of these things, fools can also be deceitful (14:8), perverse (19:1), and dishonest (10:18).

Questions

1. What is the primary reason a fool is a *fool*? _____
_____
_____

2. A common trait of a fool is his anger. Why is this a dangerous characteristic?
_____
_____
_____

3. Why can a fool be so hard to reason with? _____
_____
_____

What Fools Do: Foolish Actions & Consequences

Now that we have looked at some of the characteristics of a fool, let us explore what effect they have on themselves and others. It should not be hard to see that there is a lot of destructive behavior associated with fools, and you would naturally expect bad things to happen to them eventually. This is especially true since God has warned mankind not to act this way.

Punishment

We have noticed that fools get angry and have no respect for authority. Eventually, they will be punished by those upholding the law. Punishment in the Old Testament involved beatings and whippings, and we see that our foolish friend receives both. This is the only way to keep the fool in line since he will not listen to reason.

- "Judgments are prepared for scoffers, and beatings for the backs of fools," (Proverbs 19:29).
- "A whip for the horse, a bridle for the donkey, and a rod for the fool's back," (Proverbs 26:3). Humans need help controlling large animals, so we use bridles and whips to control their actions. Unfortunately, a fool is no better than a common beast of burden. Since he will not obey on his own, beatings must be used to force him to behave.

Disrespect

Fools will never be respected by their peers. They will not be sought after for their wisdom and will never sit with the wise rulers. His foolish words will stain his character all his days.

- "Wisdom is too lofty for a fool; he does not open his mouth in the gate," (Proverbs 24:7). The city gates were where the wise elders of a city would meet to discuss legal matters and hold court.
- "As snow in summer and rain in harvest, so honor is not fitting for a fool," (Proverbs 26:1). Just like getting snow in the summer is wrong, giving honor to fools would also be.

Shame

Wouldn't it be nice to be remembered for the good things you do upon this earth? A fool's life will only bring shame upon himself. What a sad end to any life. There are not any bedtime stories that end with the statement, "And he lived in shame until he died." Note the comparison between a wise person and fool's life: "The wise shall inherit glory, but shame shall be the legacy of fools" (Proverbs 3:35).

Death

Physical death is the ultimate end of all humans, but fools can bring a quicker end to their lives through their bad behavior.

There is also a spiritual death to be faced at the end of time. There are a lot of parallels to a fool's physical and spiritual condition where God is concerned. When tragedy comes, God gives a warning to those who will not listen to Him in Proverbs 1:28-33. Think about the application of these verses for both physical and spiritual death.

> [28] Then they will call on me, but I will not answer;
> They will seek me diligently, but they will not find me.
> [29] Because they hated knowledge
> And did not choose the fear of the Lord,
> [30] They would have none of my counsel
> And despised my every rebuke.
> [31] Therefore they shall eat the fruit of their own way,
> And be filled to the full with their own fancies.
> [32] For the turning away of the simple will slay them,
> And the complacency of fools will destroy them;
> [33] But whoever listens to me will dwell safely,
> And will be secure, without fear of evil.

Questions

4. Why did a fool need to be whipped or beaten? _____
_____
_____

5. Read Proverbs 26:7. What does this proverb mean and why? _____
_____
_____

6. Can you think of a way a fool could shorten his life? _____
   _____
   _____

7. Why would a fool suffer a spiritual death? _____
   _____
   _____

How to Deal with a Fool

God's word is clear on our relationship with fools—avoid them. There are a few simple reasons why:

1. The consequences of a fool's actions can harm others close to him. In Proverbs 17:21, 25, it tells how a fool's behavior brings great sorrow to his parents. Proverbs 13:20 warns of even greater costs: "He who walks with wise men will be wise, but the companion of fools will be destroyed."
2. The behavior of a friend who is a fool will rub off on you. Proverbs 22:24-25 warns us, "Make no friendship with an angry man, and with a furious man do not go, lest you learn his ways and set a snare for your soul." The New Testament also gives us warning about our friends. Paul stated in 1 Corinthians 15:33, "Do not be deceived: 'Evil company corrupts good habits.'"
3. A true fool will never change. Association with such a person can bring nothing but grief. God wants "broken and contrite hearts," and a fool's heart is arrogant and puffed up. A fool will not change, for he despises wisdom. Proverbs 27:22 states, "Though you grind a fool in a mortar with a pestle along with crushed grain, yet his foolishness will not depart from him."

Now, perhaps our key verse makes more sense to us all: "Do not answer a fool according to his folly, lest you also be like him" (Proverbs 26:4).

God wants us to avoid fools. Even trying to correct them is a waste of your time. They willfully turn their back on the wisdom God provides and glory in their wrongdoing. They do not change because they do not want to change. A powerful verse that demonstrates their desire to stay wrong is found in Proverbs 26:11: "As a dog returns to his own vomit, so a fool repeats his folly."

As disgusting as their lifestyle and choices are, they will continue in them until God calls them to account for their actions at the final judgment.

Questions

8. Why should you avoid a fool? _____

_____

_____

9. Name the disturbing characteristics of a fool described in Proverbs 26:10. __

_____

_____

_____

We all do foolish things in our lives, but we do not have to be fools. Proverbs 22:15 says, "Foolishness is bound up in the heart of a child; the rod of correction will drive it far from him." We all have a choice to make. Try your hardest to be like the wise man and learn from those mistakes, not like the fool who refuses to listen. Listening to and following the guidance of God's Word allows one to gain wisdom.

Lesson 7

POVERTY AND WEALTH
Our Attitude Toward the Unfortunate

When Jesus was in Bethany, a woman came to anoint His head with fragrant oil (Matthew 26:6). His disciples were very upset at this, saying, "This fragrant oil might have been sold for much and given to the poor," (26:9). But Jesus responded to them, saying, "You have the poor with you always, but me you do not have always," (26:11). He was emphasizing that the poor will always be with us on earth. Unfortunately, people can find themselves in poverty for a lot of different reasons.

Consider what Proverbs has to say regarding the causes of poverty. Sometimes, it is because of an individual's foolishness. Drinking and self-indulgence can cause poverty (Proverbs 23:21, 21:17). Laziness can cause poverty (Proverbs 20:13). Sometimes, people are poor through no fault of their own, just bad circumstances. But Jesus says no matter what the reason, there will always be poor people—which also means there will always be rich people. When we look at ourselves, we may consider ourselves as rich or poor, depending on whom we compare ourselves. No matter what we consider ourselves, there is probably someone who is poorer than we are and someone who is richer than we are. Gathering wealth is not a bad thing by itself, and neither is being poor. What matters to God is how we treat other people.

Key Verse

The rich and the poor have this in common, the Lord is the Maker of them all.

- Proverbs 22:2

Questions

1. In your own words, describe what it means to be wealthy. _____
   _____
   _____

2. In your own words, describe what it means to be poor. _____
   _____
   _____

Can you think of anyone in the Bible who was wealthy? You might think of Abraham; he was very wealthy and had many flocks and lots of silver and gold (Genesis 13:2). Job was "the greatest of all the people of the East" (Job 1:3). Then, there was King David, King Solomon, and King Hezekiah; all of these were very wealthy and righteous. The New Testament has a couple of examples as well: Joseph of Arimathea and Barnabas. All of these examples were men who loved God and lived righteously; their wealth was a blessing from God.

However, we also have examples of wealthy people who were not righteous at all. Nebuchadnezzar was king of the Babylonian Empire, but look how he used his money. He set up a huge, ninety-foot golden idol and told everyone they had to worship it or be thrown into the fiery furnace (Daniel 3:1-6). Nebuchadnezzar was prideful and self-centered, and he used his wealth wickedly. There are both good and bad people who are rich.

There are also good and bad people suffering from poverty. Whether or not we have wealth is of very little concern to God. He wants us to love Him with all our heart, but if we love gathering money more than Him, we will fall into all sorts of evil (1 Timothy 6:10). As we have seen in previous lessons, the book of Proverbs offers us Godly principles for accumulating wealth. In general, the way to gather wealth is to work hard and be thankful to God for the blessings.

Why Are Some Poor?

Sometimes, being poor is self-inflicted. Proverbs 23:21 says, "For the drunkard and the glutton will come to poverty, and drowsiness will clothe a man with rags."

Foolish choices and bad judgment often lead to expensive lessons, as can be observed from a person who chooses to drink alcohol. Buying the alcohol to get drunk is costly, and being drunk impairs judgment with any decision, leading to the destruction of property, etc. Medical expenses for injuries to yourself or others add up. Making the wrong choice to drink alcohol can lead to poverty.

Questions

3. Read the following verses and list the reasons some are poor:
   - Proverbs 21:17 _____
   _____
   - Proverbs 28:19 (Define "frivolity.") _____
   _____
   - Proverbs 24:30-34 _____
   _____
   - Proverbs 13:18 (Define "disdain.") _____
   _____

When we abandon righteousness and seek only to please our senses, it will cost us. But again consider the example of Job. We described him earlier as one of the richest men in the Bible. If you know the story of Job, you know he lost all his wealth overnight through no fault of his own (Job 1). Sometimes, people are poor because of natural disasters, severe illnesses, or mistreatment from others.

Proverbs 30:14 says:

> There is a generation whose teeth are like _____,
> And whose _____ are like knives,
> To _____ the _____ from off the earth,
> And the _____ from among men."

Proverbs 28:8 reads:

> One who _____ his possessions by usury and extortion
> Gathers it for him who will _____ the _____."

Question

7. Define "usury" and "extortion." _____
_____
_____

Whether from bad decisions, the greed and oppression of others, or simply time and chance, there will always be people who are poor.

Choices

Since there will always be those who suffer from poverty, choices about lending aid will always be present. Let us look at the advice Proverbs gives us regarding our attitude toward those who are less fortunate.

"He who gives to the poor will not lack, but he who hides his eyes will have many curses," (Proverbs 28:27). You have probably seen this happen. Some unfortunate person is on the side of the road or the sidewalk, obviously in need, while someone who could help passes by without even looking at them. Solomon describes him as "he who hides his eyes;" he will not even make eye contact with the needy person. Solomon goes on to say that person "will have many curses."

Proverbs 22:9 reads, "He who has a generous eye will be blessed, for he gives of his bread to the poor." Proverbs 14:21 also says, "He who despises his neighbor sins; but he who has mercy on the poor, happy is he." We always have a choice to make regarding the needy. God has made it clear we are to take care of our responsibilities, but when the opportunity arises, we should always be generous to others who can use some help. Jesus rebuked the Pharisees in Matthew 23:23 for not showing mercy.

The Proverbs are meant to give us principles by which to live. Do you want to be happy? Solomon says, when you live by the principle of having mercy on the poor, you will be happy. Having mercy on the poor is the same idea Jesus teaches us when He says, "It is more blessed to give than to receive" (Acts 20:35).

"He who oppresses the poor reproaches his Maker, but he who honors Him has mercy on the needy," (Proverbs 14:31). When Solomon describes God as "Maker," it reminds us that God created us all. He could have used "King," "Lord," or "God," but he used "Maker" because he made all of us in His image, none of us are any better than anyone else. We are all in need of help, and God is the only one who can supply all of us with the things we need. If God has blessed, we have a responsibility to share. But Solomon's warning goes even further; if we oppress the poor, we reproach God.

Jesus gave us a word-picture in Matthew 25:31-40 when he told His disciples about the judgment scene. God will separate the sheep from the goats with the sheep to the right and the goats to the left. He will say to those on the right,

"Come, you blessed of My Father, inherit the kingdom prepared for you..." He then describes the reason they are blessed: they fed Him when He was hungry, gave Him something to drink when he was thirsty, and gave Him a place to stay when He was homeless. Then, the blessed asks when they ever saw Him in need and when they did these things for Him. His answer is the same as Solomon teaches us in Proverbs: "Assuredly, I say to you, inasmuch as you did it to one of the least of these My brethren, you did it to Me."

But the wicked are condemned because they did not help those in need. When given a chance to help someone in need, it is just like helping Christ Himself. God made us in His image, and we are all in a lost condition without Him. We have an opportunity to help others see the blessings of faith in Jesus. If we do not share with others, we do not share anything with the Lord. Proverbs 3:9 says, "Honor the Lord with your possessions, and with the firstfruits of all your increase."

Questions

8. What does being created in the image of God have to do with our choice to help the needy? _____

   _____

9. How do you honor the Lord with your possessions? _____

   _____

   _____

10. What are "firstfruits?" _____

    _____

Who we compare ourselves to determines whether we see ourselves as poor or rich. During our lives, we may experience both extremes. Jesus instructs us in Luke 6:31, "And just as you want men to do to you, you also do to them likewise." It may be that, sometime in your life, you will need help from someone. Hopefully, they will help you as much as you have helped someone else.

Lesson 8

AWARE vs. IMPAIRED
Picking the Wise Path

Do you want to be in a situation where you are making a decision that could impact the rest of your life while only using half your brain? Sounds a bit extreme, does it not? But that is exactly the choice you make when you choose to be impaired by alcohol or other substances.

Dictionary.com defines "impaired" as "weakened, diminished, or damaged; functioning poorly or inadequately; deficient or incompetent."

The definition of impaired is not too flattering. Who would choose such a course in life? Teens face temptations regarding alcohol and drugs. It is good to remember that addiction does not happen overnight. Let us look at a real testimonial from a recovering alcoholic:

> When I was thirteen, friends would make fun of me if I didn't have a drink. I just gave in, because it was easier to join the crowd.
>
> I was really unhappy and just drank to escape my life. I went out less and less, so started losing friends. The more lonely I got, the more I drank. I was violent and out of control. I never knew what I was doing. I was ripping my family apart.
>
> Kicked out of my home at age sixteen, I was homeless and started begging for money to buy drinks. After years of abuse, doctors told me there was irreparable harm to my health.

Key Verse

Wine is a mocker, strong drink is a brawler, and whoever is led astray by it is not wise.

- Proverbs 20:1

I was only sixteen, but my liver was badly damaged, and I was close to killing myself from everything I was drinking.
– Testimonial from Samantha on DrugFreeWorld.org

Look back at Samantha's testimonial. Satan tempted her through her friends. The initial effects of drinking were probably pleasant, but notice how rapidly her life fell apart. In three short years, she had damaged her family relationships and her health. Can you see how alcohol was both a "mocker and a brawler" in her life? Alcohol's impairing effect robs you of your relationship with God.

Questions

1. What would have happened to Samantha if she had said "no" to alcohol? ___
   _____
   _____

2. Looking back, which do you think Samantha would rather have had? Her health? Or her friends? And why? _____
   _____

There were other substances besides alcohol in biblical times that people used to distort reality, but scriptural warnings are directed at the use of alcohol because it was (and still is) the most widely distributed and easily accessible drug available. We will focus on alcoholic beverages, but the principles will be the same for any substance that impairs your thought processes.

I think we can agree that God does not want us to be drunk. Both the Old and New Testaments strongly warn against this behavior. In Galatians 5:19-21, Paul says, "Now the works of the flesh are evident, which are: adultery, fornication, uncleanness, lewdness, idolatry, sorcery, hatred, contentions, jealousies, outbursts of wrath, selfish ambitions, dissensions, heresies, envy, murders, drunkenness, revelries, and the like; of which I tell you beforehand, just as I also told you in time past, that those who practice such things will not inherit the kingdom of God." Look at the sins included alongside drunkenness. God certainly hates these things.

Question

3. What did Paul tell the Galatians about those who practiced being drunk? __

_____

_____

Drunkenness (Being Drunk or Intoxicated)

Let us start exploring this subject on a note which we can all agree: being drunk causes problems. The earliest biblical example we have is connected with Noah. After surviving the flood and reaching dry land, the scripture tells us, "Noah began to be a farmer, and he planted a vineyard," (Gen. 9:20). He chose to drink the wine he produced until he was intoxicated. The story in Genesis 9 goes on to say that because of Noah's drunken actions, his son, Ham, chose to sin as well. Although there is debate on what happened, there is no debate that Noah's drunkenness caused him to be impaired to the point where his actions were foolish and caused another to sin.

Later, in Genesis 19:32-35, there is the distasteful story of Abraham's nephew Lot. After fleeing from the destruction of Sodom and Gomorrah, Lot and his two daughters lived in a cave in the mountains. His daughters devised a plan to get their father drunk, so they could get pregnant, thinking there were no other men they could marry. Their plan succeeded, and the children they produced would later become the nations of Moab and Ammon.

Both of these unfortunate stories have a common theme. Because Noah and Lot chose to be impaired by drinking alcohol, other sins happened that had lasting consequences. Noah cursed Ham, declaring that Ham's descendants would serve under his brothers' descendants. Lot's sons later became the Moabite and Ammonite people that would plague the children of Israel. Sober men would not have allowed these sins to take place. Their actions did not force anyone else to sin, but it gave others the *opportunity* to sin. Do not be a willing partner to Satan.

Questions

4. Both Noah and Lot had the choice not to do what? _____

_____

5. Are the effects of alcohol always temporary? Explain. _____
_____
_____

Soberness
(Not Being Under the Influence of Alcohol or Drugs)

Dictionary.com defines "aware" as "having knowledge or perception of a situation or fact; concerned and well-informed about a particular situation or development." Some synonyms are "mindful of," "informed about," "familiar with," "alert to," etc.

Wow! Now, that sounds like someone who is prepared to deal with life's problems. The Bible often uses the term "sober" to describe a person who is aware. Look at Peter's warning in 1 Peter 5:8: "Be sober, be vigilant; because your adversary the devil walks about like a roaring lion, seeking whom he may devour." In the cases of Noah and Lot, we saw Satan take advantage of their loack of sobriety by tempting others.

Our key verse gives a similar warning. Proverbs 20:1 states, "Wine is a mocker, strong drink is a brawler, and whoever is led astray by it is not wise." Solomon is warning against the allurement of drinking and becoming impaired. You have or will face this choice in your life. A 2014 report from the National Institute on Drug Abuse stated that 9% of eighth graders were already drinking alcohol, and the percentage shot up to 37% for twelfth graders. Solomon warns us not to be led astray.

Questions

6. Consider 1 Peter 5:8. What precautions would you take if you were being hunted by a lion? _____
_____
_____

7. The Bible says Satan is a "roaring lion," so he makes himself seen and heard. List some specific areas in your life where Satan is openly trying to impair your judgment. _____
_____

Impaired

Being impaired is not as simple a choice as being sober, drunk, or high. The dangers of drugs and alcohol (alcohol is a drug too) are subtle. Even in small amounts, drugs affect your ability to stay aware. Some studies have shown that even two glasses of wine can seriously impair your judgment and inhibit your self-control. We are now going to look at Proverbs 23:29-35, one of the longest passages in the Bible about alcohol and its effects. Read the passage now because we will be examining it in smaller chunks.

Temptation (Proverbs 23:31)

> Do not look on the wine when it is red,
> When it sparkles in the cup,
> When it swirls around smoothly...

Why do people drink? There is always an appeal to sin. In our "Wisdom & Folly" lesson, we somewhat discussed the lust of the eyes. See how Solomon described the beauty of the wine in the cup. Wine, in particular, has visual appeal, and this appeal increases after one gets accustomed to the effects it has on their bodies. Peer pressure pushes people to join in with the crowd.

Distorted Reality (Proverbs 23:33)

> Your eyes will see strange things,
> And your heart will utter perverse things.

As alcohol takes effect, your impaired judgment and brain function will play tricks on your mind. It cannot process what you see correctly, and you might even hallucinate. You cannot formulate your thoughts correctly, and you will say stupid or perverse things you normally would not. The phrase "stupid drunk" exists just for that reason; drunks often speak and act foolishly. Alcohol also lowers your defenses against doing things you know are wrong. It is like hitting the mute button on your conscience. That is why using alcohol and certain drugs causes many other sins.

Compounding Problems (Proverbs 23:29-30)

> [29] Who has woe?
> Who has sorrow?
> Who has contentions?
> Who has complaints?

> Who has wounds without cause?
> Who has redness of eyes?
> ³⁰ Those who linger long at the wine,
> Those who go in search of mixed wine.

Often, people drink to escape their problems, but alcohol offers no solutions. Those who continue using it continue in their sorrow, woes, and complaints. But now have added fighting and bruises, which they cannot remember because the alcohol deadened their senses. And they will have the reddened eyes of a heavy drinker.

Personal Endangerment (Proverbs 23:34-35a)

> ³⁴ Yes, you will be like one who lies down in the midst of the sea,
> Or like one who lies at the top of the mast, saying:
> ³⁵ "They have struck me, but I was not hurt;
> They have beaten me, but I did not feel it.'"

Heavy drinkers abuse their systems so badly that they reach a point of drunkenness where their natural defense mechanisms do not kick in, even when being beaten. They are unaware of the damage to their body because they cannot feel the pain of their injuries.

Dependency (Proverbs 23:35c)

> When shall I awake, that I may seek another drink?

Despite the harm, anguish, sorrow, and damage, they continue seeking alcohol because the relief is only temporary. The temporary relief it offers is all the alcoholic seeks. He no longer has concerns about his long-term future.

Final Outcome (Proverbs 23:32)

> At the last it bites like a serpent,
> And stings like a viper.

Satan sets his hooks deep. The effects can be permanent physical and mental damage along with spiritual death for those who continue with this behavior.

Questions

8. Name the only people who will never become alcoholics? _____
   _____

9. "If I am not drunk, I am okay." Why is this a lie? _____
   _____
   _____

Our opening testimonial from Samantha was a powerful example of what peer pressure did to a young girl and the resulting damage done in her life. Now, consider if Samantha had been a young woman with Christian faith on her side. She probably would have said "no" and gone on to find new friends that shared her values. Her example could have also helped draw others to Christ. Many young people get trapped in sinful behavior because they just want to fit in with their peers. But God wants us to be changed from the ways of the world.

Paul told the early Christians in Rome, "And do not be conformed to this world, but be transformed by the renewing of your mind, that you may prove what is that good and acceptable and perfect will of God," (Romans 12:2).

Lesson 9

PRIDE AND HUMILITY

Pride

Do you love a movie where the "stuck-up" character gets a pie in the face and everyone laughs? Why do we like to see prideful people put in their place? Often, because we know they are thinking too highly of themselves. Good thing we never do that—right?

Unfortunately, everyone struggles with pride. In fact, it is one of the three categories into which all sin falls. 1 John 2:16 says, "For all that is in the world—the lust of the flesh, the lust of the eyes, and the pride of life—is not of the Father but is of the world." Even in the Garden of Eden, Adam and Eve were tempted by Satan with a prideful statement: "Then the serpent said to the woman, 'You will not surely die. For God knows that in the day you eat of it your eyes will be opened, and you will be like God, knowing good and evil,'" (Genesis 3:4-5). Satan's temptation worked, and both Eve and Adam ate of the fruit. Did they become like God in the way Satan hinted? No, but their pride led them to believe they could be like God in all ways, and they suffered because of their actions (Genesis 3:16-24).

A prideful heart is one that tries to elevate itself. Look at Merriam-Webster's definition of pride: "a feeling of deep pleasure or satisfaction derived from one's achievements or from qualities or possessions that are widely admired." Being "prideful" is the state of being "full of pride." We call people like this "arrogant," "haughty," or "stuck up."

Key Verse

A man's pride will bring him low, but the humble in spirit will retain honor.

- Proverbs 29:23

Solomon sums up the problem of pride in Proverbs 16:18: "Pride goes before destruction and a haughty spirit before a fall."

Questions

1. What are the three categories of sin found in 1 John 2:16? _____
   _____
   _____

2. Reflecting on our key verse, how were Adam and Eve "brought low" because of their pride? (Genesis 3:23) _____
   _____
   _____

3. The knowledge Adam and Eve gained by sinning led them to feel what emotion? (Genesis 3:10) _____
   _____

Biblical Examples of Pride

We are going to look outside the book of Proverbs to other biblical figures for examples of both pride and humility. Let us start with pride.

King Uzziah (Azariah) ruled in Judah during the time of the divided kingdom (787 – 735 B.C.). He was anointed king at the age of sixteen and began his rule obeying God and doing His will. Read 2 Chronicles 26:4-5.

Sounds like a great start, right? It was. He went on to rule a total of 52 years, and Judah counted him as a good king. If you read the entire account of his life in 2 Chronicles, you will see the many advances he made for the kingdom because God was with him. So, what could go wrong? Pride.

"But when he was strong his heart was lifted up, to his destruction, for he transgressed against the Lord his God by entering the temple of the Lord to burn incense on the altar of incense," (2 Chronicles 26:16).

Even a righteous king like Uzziah could be tempted by Satan's old trick of pride. As happens so often, when someone achieves great success, they begin to think it is all done with their own hands, and discount the existence of God in the matter. Satan's whispers are then, "Who needs God? You did this all by yourself!" Note how the scripture above says "his heart was lifted up." Just like the definition of pride we saw, his heart was full of pride for the things he had done. So much so that he took it upon himself to enter the temple and burn incense, which was a duty restricted by God to be done only by the priests, who were from the tribe of Levi (see Exodus 28 and 29). All the kings of Judah descended through the line of David and were from the tribe of Judah.

Uzziah's arrogance cost him dearly, for as the priests were telling him of his sin, he grew angry at them instead of being sorry for what he had done. God chose to "bring him low" by striking the king with leprosy. Not only would this disease cost him his life, but he was unclean because of it and was never able to enter the temple of God again during his lifetime (2 Chronicles 26:21).

Questions

4. Who is tempted by pride? _____
   _____
   _____

5. Look up leprosy and its effects. List some of the symptoms King Uzziah may have faced. _____
   _____
   _____

6. Who struck Uzziah with leprosy? Why? _____
   _____
   _____

Humility

The second part of our key verse is the opposite of pride. It is about humility: "But the humble in spirit will retain honor," (Proverbs 29:23b). So, what is humility, and why does God want his children to be humble?

Strong's definition of humility is, "having a humble opinion of oneself; a deep sense of one's (moral) littleness; modesty, humility, lowliness of mind." Wow, it is the opposite of pride. God values this trait in both the Old and New Testaments. Here are a few more verses from Proverbs emphasizing the importance of being humble:

- "When pride comes, then comes shame; but with the humble is wisdom," (Proverbs 11:2).
- "The fear of the Lord is the instruction of wisdom, and before honor is humility," (Proverbs 15:33).
- "By humility and the fear of the Lord are riches and honor and life," (Proverbs 22:4).

So, why would God want us to be humble? Think about it this way: have you ever stood at the edge of the seashore, on top of a mountain, or on the edge of a cliff? It should make you feel like you are a speck in this big world. Psalms 19:1 states, "The heavens declare the glory of God; and the firmament shows His handiwork." Now, consider that God made all these things with His word alone. How would you expect God to want His creation to act toward Him? If your answer is, "With awe and humility," you are on the right track.

Questions

7. Based on Proverbs, list some of the possible benefits of having humility. ___
___
___

8. What aspects of nature point toward God as the creator? ___
___
___

Biblical Examples of Humility

Moses

A great example of humility is Moses. Numbers 12:3 says, "the man Moses was very humble, more than all men who were on the face of the earth." Moses spent the first 40 years of his life in the household of Pharaoh—hardly a humble beginning. But he spent the next 40 years of his life shepherding sheep in the land of Midian (Exodus 3:1). God was preparing this man to shepherd His children out of the land of Egypt. God needed a leader with a humble heart because he would be performing incredible miracles in the land of Egypt. Moses knew he was an instrument of God and gave Him the glory.

Paul

The New Testament gives us the apostle Paul, who had quite a start. Acts 22:3 states, "I am indeed a Jew, born in Tarsus of Cilicia, but brought up in this city at the feet of Gamaliel, taught according to the strictness of our fathers' law, and was zealous toward God as you all are today." Paul's zeal led him to persecute Christians until Jesus struck him blind on the road to Damascus. After his conversion to Christ, we still see Paul had a zeal for God, but his opinion of himself had been humbled.

Paul called himself the chief sinner (1 Timothy 1:15), the least of the apostles (1 Corinthians 15:9), and less than the least of all saints (Ephesians 3:8). He dedicated his life to doing the will of God and continually gave Him the glory. Paul said of his labors in 1 Corinthians 15:10, "But by the grace of God I am what I am, and His grace toward me was not in vain; but I labored more abundantly than they all, yet not I, but the grace of God which was with me."

Questions

9. True or False: Both Moses and Paul started from humble beginnings. _____

10. Paul was able to do great things because what was with him? _____
_____

11. Moses' humility toward his ability to speak caused God to allow Aaron to do what for Moses? (Exodus 4:16) _____
_____

The embodiment of pride exists in Satan. The book of Isaiah (14:12-15) hints at his fall from Heaven.

> [12] How you are fallen from heaven,
> O Lucifer, son of the morning!
> How you are cut down to the ground,
> You who weakened the nations!
> [13] For you have said in your heart:
> "I will ascend into heaven,
> I will exalt my throne above the stars of God;

> I will also sit on the mount of the congregation
> On the farthest sides of the north;
> [14] I will ascend above the heights of the clouds,
> I will be like the Most High."
> [15] Yet you shall be brought down to Sheol,
> To the lowest depths of the Pit.

God hates pride and it separates us from Him. Do not allow Satan to tempt you into following his fate.

Jesus Himself is the ultimate example of becoming humble to do God's will. "Let this mind be in you which was also in Christ Jesus, who, being in the form of God, did not consider it robbery to be equal with God, but made Himself of no reputation, taking the form of a bondservant, and coming in the likeness of men. And being found in appearance as a man, He humbled Himself and became obedient to the point of death, even the death of the cross," (Phil. 2:5-8).

Just as God exalted Christ, so shall we be exalted if we put away our prideful hearts and humble ourselves in the sight of the Lord.

Lesson 10

A WORTHY WOMAN
How to Find One—or Be One

Morality vs. Immorality

Have you ever watched an elderly married couple at church? Do you wonder how they have been able to stay together so long? It must be hard when the world is constantly trying to tear down family values. The answer is a simple one: both the man and the woman made a wise choice on who to marry, along with honoring their commitment.

In an earlier lesson, we learned there is a battle between wisdom and folly, with each often represented as women in Proverbs. Proverbs was written specifically with young men in mind but young ladies along with older men and women can still learn from God's inspired word. Proverbs was written as advice on the more practical aspects of life. Since all scripture is inspired and profitable (2 Timothy 3:16), everyone should study and apply the lessons Proverbs provides.

With that in mind, the young ladies in class can use one of two methods during this lesson to help them get the most out of this important study. First, you may be able to mentally reverse the gender in a verse to help you see the application for you. For example, Proverbs 11:22 says, "As a ring of gold in a swine's snout, so is a lovely woman who lacks discretion." You could think of the last line as, "So is a handsome man who lacks discretion." No woman should want to marry a man who's a fool. The second method is to place yourself in the role of

Key Verse

He who finds a wife finds a good thing, and obtains favor from the Lord.

- Proverbs 18:22

the woman Wisdom. What qualities does God think are important? How should a righteous woman attract a righteous man? _____
_____

Proverbs can be a guidebook for women on how to be pleasing to God and how to find the right kind of man for a lasting relationship.

God wants stable and lasting marriages. In Jesus' teaching on marriage and divorce in Matthew, he states, "Therefore what God has joined together, let not man separate," (Matthew 19:6b).

Questions

1. In Matthew 19, when did Jesus say marriage was started by God? _____
   _____

2. What book of the Bible contains practical wisdom for everyday living? _____
   _____

3. Why can females not just ignore Proverbs since it was written for young men?
   _____
   _____

Seeking the Right Woman

Just as we are to seek wisdom and avoid folly, so should a young man look for the right girl and avoid the immoral ones. Many of you may not have had a boyfriend or girlfriend yet, but you have all made friendships with members of the opposite sex. What types of friends do you make? _____
_____

Boys, if you are drawn to girls who are immodest in what they wear, do not care about going to church, or do not worry about their grades, you may be hanging around girls who are not concerned about becoming "wise women."

Girls, if you find yourself wanting to wear clothes or makeup which do not meet with parental approval, pretending to not be interested in church, pretending not to go to church as often as you do, or you are always thinking the bad boys in class are funny and cute, you could be sending the signal that you are not a moral and godly girl.

Of course, people can change, and these thoughts may not always be true, but just like Proverbs, these generalizations have proven true for centuries. When you reach the age when your parents will allow you to date, keep in mind that the ultimate goal of your dating years is to find a mate for life. It is wise to set a standard for the type of people you date. One important characteristic that Proverbs teaches is seeking the wisdom of God.

Proverbs 1:7 says, "The fear of the Lord is the beginning of knowledge, but fools despise wisdom and instruction." The writer of Proverbs drives home the importance of seeking wisdom in the first nine chapters and consequently implies we should seek women or men who possess this quality. His strong warnings against immoral women focus on prostitutes and adulterous wives, but the principles of committing immoral acts result in the same damage to one's soul.

Some of the warnings against the Immoral Woman include:
- She seeks out the simple and inexperienced (Proverbs 7:7).
- Seeking her out can lead to poverty (Proverbs 6:25).
- She desires sexual relations outside of marriage (Proverbs 7:19).
- Her path leads to death (Proverbs 5:5).

With so many warnings, who would ever consider being tempted by the Immoral Woman? Answer: young men. Young ladies are not immune from the same type of temptation either. As teens reach maturity, there is a great temptation to ignore God's law. It is possible to stay faithful to God's desire for us to remain pure until marriage. Joseph serves as a great role model for purity.

Joseph faced the choice of obeying God or caving into temptation. The story of Potiphar's wife continually inviting him to sin with her is found in Genesis 39. Potiphar was the captain of the guard for Pharaoh and, therefore, a man of status and means. There is no reason to believe his wife was old and ugly; on the contrary, she was most likely quite beautiful. But when faced with the temptation of the adulterous wife, Joseph's response was, "How could I do such a wicked thing? It would be a great sin against God" (Genesis 39:9b).

Questions

4. Where does true knowledge begin? _____
   _____

5. How many times did Joseph have to refuse the advances of Potiphar's wife?
   _____
   _____

6. What is the ultimate goal of your dating years? _____
   _____
   _____

The Virtuous Woman (Proverbs 31:10-31)

The Proverbs writer dedicates the last verses to a description of the Virtuous (or Worthy) Woman. These verses are an excellent place for both males and females to see what God finds beautiful in a woman. Unlike the foolish woman who pulls down her house with her own hands, this Virtuous Woman builds it up.

Notice some of the qualities God finds worthwhile.

- She manages her home well. Popular culture looks down on women who choose to be "just a housewife." But look at the skill and effort this woman uses for her home:
    - She purchases food from near and far (31:14).
    - She checks over the quality of her goods (31:18).
    - She provides the household with proper garments (31:21).
    - She monitors what is going on in her home (31:27).
    - By doing these tasks, she is a true helper to her husband. He was known at the gates of the city where the leaders met to convene court, make business transactions, and proclaim public announcements. Since he made a wise choice for a wife and because she managed their home so well, he was respected and could participate as a leader of the city (31:23).

- She is a worker and never lazy:
  - She buys wool and flax, which are materials to make fabric for clothing and other needs and does the work herself (31:13, 19).
  - She is up early, making sure the household has food for the day (31:15).
  - She is a woman of industry, who understands business and buys and sells goods (31:15, 18, 24).

- She is generous to the needy (31:20).

- She keeps herself physically and spiritually strong for the work she needs to do (31:25, 26).

- She is loved and respected by her family (31:28).

One can learn many other lessons from this woman. Notice what she is worth to her husband in verse 10: "For her worth is far above rubies." So, even beyond earthly wealth, this woman will make their married life wonderful.

Questions

Refer to Proverbs 31:10-31.

7. Where does physical beauty rate as far as God's concerned? _____
   _____
   _____

8. How long will she be good to her husband? _____
   _____

9. What will a woman who fears the Lord receive? _____
   _____
   _____

It may seem like you are receiving this lesson too early for your stage in life, but Proverbs provides so many lessons for young men and women approaching adulthood. Since many of you could be married soon, it is wise to be the right kind of person and to look for the right kind of perseon who will make a great mate. You can greatly increase your chances of having a fulfilled and contented life by listening to God's wisdom.

Lesson 11

AUTHORITY

Key Verse

The Lord by wisdom founded the earth; by understanding He established the heavens.

- Proverbs 3:19

Picture in your mind blue lights flashing and sirens screaming. Someone is driving too fast, and the police are chasing him down to give him a ticket. The officer, dressed in his dark blue uniform with matching hat, gets out of his police cruiser and starts walking toward the speeder's car. The officer has on dark sunglasses, and his badge gleams in the sunlight. He asks for the driver's license and says, "Do you know how fast you were going?"

Likely, you have seen this happen several times on TV shows, maybe even in real life. Have you ever wondered who gets to decide what the speed limit is? Or why the police officer gets to say who is going too fast? What or who gives them the right to say anything about how someone drives? Who gives them their authority? These are important questions.

There are many other similar questions we have concerning authority. Questions like:
- Why should I listen to my parents?
- Why should I obey my teachers?
- Do I really have to follow the laws of the government?
- Do I even have to follow corrupt governments?
- Who gives anyone the right to say something about what someone else does?
- Who gives anyone authority anyway?

All around us, there are people who do not respect the police. We see people who disrespect their school teachers, their principal, and anyone else in authority. We need to know where authority comes from and why we should respect those in positions of authority. The book of Proverbs has a lot to say about this subject.

Question

1. Define "authority." _____
_____
_____

What Is Authority?

It all begins with God. Let us take another look at our key verse, Proverbs 3:19: "The Lord by wisdom founded the earth; by understanding, He established the heavens."

You are familiar with Genesis 1:1, "In the beginning, God created the heavens and the earth." Solomon says in Proverbs 3 that God used *wisdom* to create everything and it was God's *understanding* that *established the heavens*. Because of God's power, knowledge, and wisdom, He made everything and is in control of everything.

In all of our lessons, we have been looking at the difference between wisdom and foolishness. In Proverbs 8, Solomon gives the woman Wisdom a voice. Beginning in verse one, she calls out for all to listen and tells them the blessings that come to those who listen to her. Then, she describes how important wisdom was in the creation of all things. Look at Proverbs 8:22-23:

> [22] The Lord possessed me at the beginning of his work.
> The first of his acts of old
> [23] Ages ago I was set up,
> At the first, before the beginning of the earth.

Solomon describes God using wisdom to make the mountains, the fields, and the dust of the earth. It was with wisdom that He made the heavens, seas, and everything else. Proverbs 8:30-31 says:

> [30] Then I [wisdom] was beside him, like a master workman,
> And I was daily his delight, rejoicing before him always,
> [31] Rejoicing in his inhabited world
> And delighting in the children of man."

It was through wisdom that God made man and "the children of man." He made us. He also made us in His image (Gen 1:26-27). He is the Creator. The fact that He has the power to do all that means He has all the authority. He deserves our respect and worship. He deserves our obedience.

Question

2. Using Proverbs 20:12, explain why God has the authority? _____
_____
_____

Agents of Authority

Government

Since God is the creator of all things and we should obey Him, what does that have to do with obeying the government, the police, or even mom and dad? The answer to that is almost the same as the question. Since God is the Creator and we obey Him, we must obey the people to whom He has given authority. God has passed on certain powers and authority to others here on earth. Proverbs 8:15-16 states:

> [15] By me kings reign,
> And rulers decree what is just;
> [16] By me princes rule,
> And nobles, all who govern justly."

God has established all the governments—every king, every prime minister, every president. That does not mean that every government is righteous or that they even believe in God. But it does mean God has given them authority. Unless it causes us to violate God's law, we must recognize their authority.

Remember how God used evil King Nebuchadnezzar? He was not a righteous king, but Daniel told him, "You, O King, are a king of kings. For the God of heaven has given you a kingdom, power, strength, and glory" (Daniel 2:37). God put Nebuchadnezzar on the throne and used him to punish the Israelites by taking them into captivity. It is God who controls all things, even national governments like Babylon. They are His representatives for justice. He placed them in authority, so we must respect them. Solomon says some will be good leaders and some will not. Proverbs 29:2 reads:

> When the righteous are in authority,
> The people rejoice;
> But when a wicked man rules,
> The people groan.

It is nice when we have good, God-fearing leaders, but that is sometimes not the case. Jesus came to Earth during Roman rule, which was marked by forced brutality, idolatry, and corruption. Whether good or bad, governments are the authority God has chosen for us. Whether they are righteous or wicked, God uses them to His glory.

Police

Once we understand that God has established governments and given them authority to rule here on Earth, it is easy to recognize the role of the police. Police agencies receive their authority to uphold the laws of the land from the government. They make sure people comply with the law. They also protect us from people who break the law. Sometimes, laws are made to keep everyone safe, like the speed limit in a school zone. We must respect policemen because they are doing a job God designed for our benefit (Romans 13:1-7). If we break laws, disobey the police, and reject the authority of the government, then we deny the authority of God and will suffer the consequences.

Questions

3. Using Romans 13:4, explain what Solomon was talking about in Proverbs 24:21.

   _____
   _____
   _____

4. Since God established governments and rulers, why are some rulers evil (like Nebuchadnezzar)? _____

   _____
   _____
   _____

Parents

Just as God established governments, God designed the family. His plan is for a man and a woman to marry and have children (Gen 1:27-28). But this relationship between parents and children is much more than just "multiplying and subduing the earth." This relationship is essential for our spiritual well-being (and will be covered in detail in an upcoming lesson). God designed it so we could learn how to live in this world and know about Him. Our parents feed us when we are too young to feed ourselves. They give us shelter and clothing. They teach us how to walk and talk. They help us grow up strong and wise. They teach us to do the right thing all the time.

Proverbs 28:6 says, "Better is the poor who walks in his integrity than one perverse in his ways, though he be rich." Giving us instruction is the responsibility God gave to our parents. He has granted them the authority to rule over us while in their home. They are to teach us the way to God because they love us and because it is what God expects of them.

Proverbs 22:6 also reads, "Train up a child in the way he should go, and when he is old he will not depart from it." Our parents deserve our respect because God gave them the authority to teach and correct us. They also send us to other teachers for instruction. We go to Bible class to gain knowledge from other Christians. We listen to sermons in worship to hear God's word. We go to school to learn math, science, and language. All of these teachers are here for our good, and all of them deserve our respect and honor because God put them in our lives to guide us.

Questions

5. List at least five ways you can show honor to your parents. _____
   _____
   _____
   _____

6. Using Proverbs 20:20, explain what will happen to the child who does not love and obey his parents. _____
   _____
   _____

7. Using Proverbs 19:20, explain how a young person can be wise when they get older. _____
_____
_____

God is the creator of all things, and He made us in His image. He made the president in His image, and He made the police officers in His image. He made our parents, Bible class teacher, preacher, elders, and school teachers all in His image. He also gave authority to them in different parts of our lives. He did all of this to help us grow closer to Him. If we fail to respect people who God put in our lives to guide and teach us, then we fail to respect God. All authority begins and ends with God.

Lesson 12

SEEING JESUS IN PROVERBS

During this study, you might have wondered, "This is all interesting, but what's it got to do with our spiritual life now? Aren't we supposed to follow Jesus?" Yes we are, but the Old Testament plays a key role in the lives of God's children, even today. In this lesson, we will take a look at the importance of the Old Testament scripture and see a glimpse of Jesus in Proverbs.

Why Study the Old Testament?

Have you ever started watching a movie when it was more than halfway over? Can you figure out what is going on without asking questions? You can probably get the gist of the story, but will the ending have as full a meaning to you if you do not know the backstory? Of course not, and the Old Testament is the key backstory for the events in the New Testament. But many Christians only bother to study the New Testament passages. This is a mistake for those who truly want to understand God's word.

In 2 Timothy, it tells us, "All Scripture is given by inspiration of God, and is profitable for doctrine, for reproof, for correction, for instruction in righteousness, that the man of God may be complete, thoroughly equipped for every good work" (2 Tim. 3:16-17).

When Paul wrote these words to Timothy, the New Testament had not been completed. In fact, the Old Testament makes up about seventy five percent of God's total message to humans. Jesus often quoted the Old Testament

Key Verse

For whoever finds me finds life, and obtains favor from the Lord...

– Proverbs 8:35

in his teachings. Almost one third of the New Testament writings are quotes or allusions to Old Testament scripture. So, what purpose did the Old Testament serve for the first-century Christians? Paul gives us a hint in Galatians 3:24: "Therefore the law was our tutor to bring us to Christ, that we might be justified by faith."

The Old Testament still serves as a tutor for us today, explaining all the events of the Bible that led to Jesus coming to Earth. Jesus proved this after his resurrection when speaking to the disciples on the road to Emmaus: "And beginning at Moses and all the Prophets, He expounded to them in all the Scriptures the things concerning Himself" (Luke 24:27). God's plan was made complete in Jesus. It is said that "the Old Testament is God's will concealed, and the New Testament is God's will revealed." It is impossible to grasp the full meaning of God's eternal plan without exploring and learning all of His inspired writings to mankind.

Is Jesus in the Proverbs?

The original audience (Solomon's sons and the children of Israel) would not have seen or looked for the Messiah (God's chosen one) in Proverbs. They recognized the theme we have discussed—that there is a choice between wisdom and folly. They also knew that Wisdom represented God and Folly stood for the idols that turned the peoples' hearts away from God.

Although there are no obvious messianic prophesies (predictions about Jesus coming as the Messiah) in Proverbs, we might be able to catch glimpses of Him. Have you ever watched a movie a second time and noticed new things? That is because you know the ending and see clues that point to the conclusion you did not notice previously. The same is true for Christians today. We have the benefit of seeing the whole biblical story laid out before us and are therefore able to catch hints of Jesus throughout the Old Testament. In Proverbs, this is especially true as it relates to Wisdom. Closer examination of the life of Jesus shows an interesting relationship between Him and Wisdom.

Questions

1. Why is all scripture profitable for study, even the Old Testament? _____

_____

_____

2. Where in the scriptures did Jesus go to teach about Himself on the road to Emmaus? _____
_____

3. The Old Testament makes up about how much of the total Bible? _____
_____

4. Choosing wisdom was the same as choosing what? _____
_____

Glimpses of Wisdom in Jesus' Youth

Even at the beginning of Jesus' life, wisdom is mentioned. From far away, wise men sought the King who was heralded in the stars. Matthew 2:1-2 says, "Now after Jesus was born in Bethlehem of Judea in the days of Herod the king, behold, wise men from the East came to Jerusalem, saying, 'Where is He who has been born King of the Jews? For we have seen His star in the East and have come to worship Him.'"

Not much is told of Jesus as a boy, but the one mention of Him at twelve years old showed He had already gained wisdom. The story in Luke 2:41-50 tells of the family of Jesus going to Jerusalem for the Passover. After the celebration, they were headed back to Nazareth with a large group and discovered Jesus was not with any of the other families. After searching for Him three days in Jerusalem, they found Him with the teachers in the temple, not only listening but also asking questions. Verse 47 says, "And all who heard Him were astonished at His understanding and answers." Jesus already exhibited the wisdom of God. Luke 2:52 also states, "And Jesus increased in wisdom and stature, and in favor with God and men."

Glimpses of Wisdom in Jesus' Ministry

One of the main teaching methods Jesus used during His preaching was parables. It is interesting that the Hebrew word for "*proverb*" (mashal) is the same Greek word for "*parable*" (parabole). There is obvious wisdom in the parables, even in the superficial meaning of the stories. But Jesus taught a deeper, spiritual meaning to his disciples. Jesus was a teacher of wisdom, and this was acknowledged by those who heard Him. Mark 6:2 states, "And when the Sabbath had come, He began to teach in the synagogue. And many hearing Him were astonished, saying, 'Where did this Man get these things? And what wisdom is this which is given to Him, that such mighty works are performed by His hands!'"

But Jesus is so much more than just a teacher of wisdom; He is the embodiment (visible form) of Wisdom. Solomon was given wisdom by God Himself. In 1 Kings 3:12, God said, "I have given you a wise and understanding heart, so that there has not been anyone like you before you, nor shall any like you arise after you." As the wisest man on earth and with God's inspiration, Solomon penned the wisdom literature of the Old Testament, including Proverbs. But as great as Solomon was, Jesus said there was One greater: Himself.

Matthew 12:42 says, "The queen of the South will rise up in the judgment with this generation and condemn it, for she came from the ends of the earth to hear the wisdom of Solomon; and indeed a greater than Solomon is here."

Of course, there is only one way Jesus could surpass the God-given wisdom of Solomon, and He tells us it is because of His relationship with God. In John 10:30, Jesus proclaims, "I and My Father are one."

Questions

5. When Jesus' parents found Him in the temple at age twelve, whose business did He say He was doing? Who exactly did He mean? _____

_____

_____

6. In Mark 6:2, why should the people have known the wisdom of Jesus came from God? _____

_____

7. Looking at 1 Kings 10, why did the Queen of Sheba (of the South) come to visit Solomon? What was her conclusion after her visit? _____

_____

_____

Glimpses of Wisdom from the Son of God

We have discussed Proverbs 8 since it is one of the passages that personifies wisdom as a woman. In the New Testament, there are several parallel scriptures that point to Jesus as Wisdom. The Wisdom in Proverbs 8 is described as *divine*, *the source of life*, *righteous*, and *available to those who will receive it*. These are the same qualities Jesus possesses throughout the New Testament.

Let us explore some of the similarities between Jesus and the woman Wisdom in Proverbs 8. Do not be confused by the structure of poetry in Proverbs when Wisdom is portrayed as a woman. Remember, the target audience was young men. Ultimately, the Wisdom in Proverbs is always describing God.

In Proverbs 8, it says Wisdom was with God during the creation. "The Lord possessed me at the beginning of His way, before His works of old. I have been established from everlasting, from the beginning, before there was ever an earth" (Proverbs 8:22-23).

Now, compare those two verses with the language in John 1:1-3: "In the beginning was the Word, and the Word was with God, and the Word was God. He was in the beginning with God. All things were made through Him, and without Him nothing was made that was made," (John 1:1-3).

Look at our key verse, Proverbs 8:35, which says: "For whoever finds me finds life, and obtains favor from the Lord..." Compare our key verse to Jesus' statement in John 14:6: "Jesus said to him, 'I am the way, the truth, and the life. No one comes to the Father except through Me.'"

The apostle Paul also confirms that Jesus is God's Wisdom in 1 Corinthians 1:30: "But of Him you are in Christ Jesus, who became for us wisdom from God."

The message of Proverbs is for us to choose wisdom or folly—God or idols. The message Jesus gives us today is also about a choice we all have to make: choose God or Satan. As the Son of God, Jesus was living wisdom and deity among men. He presented the choice that each person must make in His Sermon on the Mount (Matthew 7:24-27):

> [24] Therefore whoever hears these sayings of Mine, and does them, I will liken him to a wise man who built his house on the rock: [25] and the rain descended, the floods came, and the winds blew and beat on that house; and it did not fall, for it was founded on the rock.

²⁶ But everyone who hears these sayings of Mine, and does not do them, will be like a foolish man who built his house on the sand: ²⁷ and the rain descended, the floods came, and the winds blew and beat on that house; and it fell. And great was its fall.

Questions

8. Do we have to worry about choosing between God and idols today? _____
   _____

9. How was Jesus able to become Wisdom on the Earth? _____
   _____
   _____

10. What is the only choice a wise person will make concerning God? _____
    _____
    _____

Lesson 13

AWE FOR GOD

Fear & Awe

We have seen that the book of Proverbs gives sound, godly advice about things we face every day. It instructs us on how to live righteously in this life and how to make the right choices in any given situation. Together, we have learned about friends and neighbors, rich and poor, and honoring authority. We have also studied money issues, parent-child relationships, and how to win the battle between wisdom and folly. Over and over, Proverbs shows us that it is better to choose wisdom instead of foolishness.

Central to all of these instructions is the "fear of the Lord." What is the "fear" we are to have? Is it just being afraid of God? Of course not. It is a natural fear that comes from an awe for God. Dictionary.com defines "awe" as "an overwhelming feeling of reverence, admiration, fear, etc., produced by that which is grand, sublime, extremely powerful, or the like." The psalmist in Psalms 33:6, 8 captures how fear and awe work together:

> [6] By the word of the Lord the heavens were made...
> [8] Let all the earth fear the Lord;
> Let all the inhabitants of the world stand in awe of Him.

God is grand and extremely powerful. His greatness demands our reverence. These counsels give us direction in life, and they teach us that our lives are in God's hands.

Key Verse

The fear of the Lord is the beginning of wisdom, and the knowledge of the Holy One is understanding.

– Proverbs 9:10

When we follow God's laws, we will usually have longer, happier, more successful lives in this world. How do we know this? Consider what Solomon says in Proverbs 19:23: "The fear of the Lord leads to life, and he who has it will abide in satisfaction; he will not be visited with evil."

Having fear and awe for God will motivate us to do the right thing. But it is much more than just contentment in this life; it is the path to eternal life as well. Proverbs 14:27 says, "The fear of the Lord is a fountain of life, to turn one away from the snares of death."

Thought Questions

1. Read Proverbs 10:27. In your own words, explain why "the fear of the Lord prolongs days." _____
   _____
   _____

2. Read Proverbs 9:10. Where do we gain "knowledge of the Holy One?" _____
   _____

The Loss of Awe

The world we live in is losing its respect, its *awe* for God. Unfortunately, we can see this happen often in God's word. Adam lost respect for God's commandment, and God expelled him from the garden (Genesis 3). The entire world thought *evil continually* during the time of Noah, so God destroyed them (Genesis 6-8). The Israelites stopped honoring God and began worshipping gods of their design until God allowed their enemies to take them into captivity (2 Chronicles 36:15-17). Also, in the Book of Revelation, the church at Ephesus was rebuked because they had *left their first love* (Revelation 2:4).

We are witnessing a moral decline in our culture; we see it in the use of vulgar language (including the improper use of God's name), in the way people dress, and in the poor choices they make for entertainment. How does this happen? It happens when we lose respect for God's authority. When we stop having reverence for the greatness of God and lose the fear of the extreme powerfulness of God, we have lost awe for God. When we do not have awe for God, we replace it with a feeling of awe for ourselves. This is called arrogance.

Proverbs speaks about this attitude. Proverbs 8:13 says, "The fear of the Lord is to hate evil; pride and arrogance and the evil way and the perverse mouth I hate." Also, Proverbs 21:24 reads, "A proud and haughty man—'Scoffer' is his name; he acts with arrogant pride."

Questions

3. Define "scoffer." _____
_____
_____

4. Define "arrogance." _____
_____
_____

The Arrogant Answer

The problem with pride and arrogance is they steal the awe from you and replace it with self-assured lies. Pride causes us to rely too much on ourselves. Pride is the opposite of awe for God; "Pride goes before destruction" (Proverbs 16:18). Solomon says the *proud and haughty man* has a name, and his name is *Scoffer*. The New King James Version of the Scriptures uses the word scoffer 15 times, and 13 of the 15 times are in the book of Proverbs. The warnings are abundant. Now that you have defined it, you know *The Scoffer* is a person who mocks God and has contempt for his word—no awe for the Creator.

Question

5. What is the difference between pride and being proud of something or someone? _____
_____
_____
_____

Pride and arrogance look to self for the answers to life's challenges. Pride is the exact opposite of *fear the Lord*. If we are going to honor God with the reverence and respect He is due, it must begin with a humble heart.

Awe Begins with Humility

Have you ever met someone famous or important? Perhaps you have had a chance to meet a mayor, governor, or professional athlete. What if you received an invitation to visit the White House and meet the president? How would you act? Hopefully, you would be on your best behavior, because you would want to make a good impression. We can understand showing respect and honor to an important person. We can also understand being nervous when you meet them. If we have these emotions when it comes to humans, what about when it comes to God? How would it be meeting with Him? Luckily, the Bible records people's reactions to having contact with God. Let us take a look and see what we can learn.

In Exodus 19, after Moses led the Israelites out of Egypt, they came to Mount Sinai where He received the law. They had seen God's miraculous power in the plagues, crossing the Red Sea, the manna from Heaven, and water from a rock. But when God gave them the law, speaking directly to them in His voice, it terrified them to the point of death. They begged Moses to speak to God on their behalf because they feared the Lord.

In Isaiah 6, the prophet describes his experience: "I saw the Lord sitting on a throne, high and lifted up, and the train of His robe filled the temple...So I said: 'Woe is me, for I am undone! Because I am a man of unclean lips, and I dwell in the midst of a people of unclean lips; for my eyes have seen the King, the Lord of hosts.'" (6:1, 5).

Our last example is the apostle John's record of his vision in Revelation 1:17. He says, "And when I saw Him, I fell at His feet as dead. But He laid His right hand on me, saying to me, 'Do not be afraid; I am the First and the Last.'" All of these responses—by the Israelites, Isaiah, and John—show an immense reverence and respect for the majestic glory of God. Each humbled themselves in the presence of unmatched power. That is *awe*.

Discovering Your Awe

Have you ever been *awe-inspired*? Is there something you have witnessed in this life that has humbled your heart to realize you are just a tiny part of a vast universe? Perhaps it has happened on a mountain trail or while viewing a natural wonder, like the Grand Canyon or a desert. Maybe it has happened while you sat on a beach, contemplating the ocean and marveling at the immensity of the water.

There are an infinite variety of complexities in the universe, from the smallest microscopic particle to the largest mammal—from the mechanics of tidal action to the balance of plant and animal life. Think of the design and how incredible it is. Now, how much more should we be impressed by the Designer? God made all that we see. With a word, He spoke it into existence (Genesis 1). With His breath, He breathed life into each of us. Does that humble you? "Our God is an awesome God!"

Solomon recounts the creation account from Genesis 1 in poetic language that helps us realize the vastness of God's power. Proverbs 3:19-20 says, "The Lord by wisdom founded the earth; by understanding He established the heavens; by His knowledge the depths were broken up, and clouds drop down the dew."

Questions

6. Based on the verses above, what were the key qualities with God during the creation? _____
_____

7. In your own words, describe something in creation that causes you to appreciate the power of God. _____
_____

8. Stake out an area, and take note of all the life you can observe—from the crawling insects to the birds above. Note the different types of vegetation and fungi. Think about the creatures you cannot even see that are alive in the soil and under the earth. Document what you observed and describe the wonder you witnessed. _____
_____
_____

How Should Our Actions Reflect Our Awe for God?

What does this mean to us in practical terms? How do we begin to offer the kind of honor God is due? This entire study has been about the choice each human must make: will I follow God or Satan? God offers wisdom, a fulfilled life, and eternal rewards. Satan offers temporary pleasure combined with strife, chaos, and eternal punishment. On the printed page, it seems like a simple answer, but in real life, the allurements of sin sway many, young and old, to fall.

Think back to the scenario of being invited to meet with the President of the United States. How would you dress and act? You would clean yourself up, wear your best clothes, and possibly bring a gift to present him. Do you take that much effort now for your Creator? Do you look and act your best for Him? Do you study your Bible for class? Do you present yourself as a living sacrifice in honor of all He has done? How should we act to show we are truly in awe of God? Jesus gives a clear message in John 15:10: "If you keep My commandments, you will abide in My love, just as I have kept My Father's commandments and abide in His love."

The apostle Paul told the brethren at Thessalonica to "pray without ceasing" (1 Thessalonians 5:7). Prayer is an essential step to loving God with all your heart. Pray for wisdom like Solomon, and keep yourself from situations where you will be tempted to act immorally. Do not listen to the call of Folly, who will lead you to sin and death. Listen instead to Wisdom, who will help lead you down the path of righteousness and life.

Questions

9. Read Revelation 15:4. Who will come to fear the Lord? _____

_____

10. What happened to the children of Israel when they no longer feared or obeyed the Lord? (See Deuteronomy 28:58-63.) List the consequences God promised.

_____

_____

_____

_____

_____

It all begins and ends with God. If we are going to be wise and knowledgeable, we must humble ourselves and stand in awe of the only God of heaven. Grace be with you on your journey.

"The fear of the Lord is the beginning of knowledge..." (Proverbs 1:7).

www.ingramcontent.com/pod-product-compliance
Lightning Source LLC
Chambersburg PA
CBHW070627050426
42450CB00011B/3139